THE HOLY GRAIL

THE
HOLY GRAIL
HISTORY AND LEGEND

Juliette Wood

UNIVERSITY OF WALES PRESS
CARDIFF
2012

www.uwp.co.uk

British Library CIP Data
A catalogue record for this book is available from the British Library

ISBN   978-0-7083-2524-7
e-ISBN 978-0-7083-2525-4

The right of Juliette Wood to be identified as author of this work has been asserted in accordance with sections 77 and 79 of the Copyright, Designs and Patents Act 1988.

Designed and typeset by Chris Bell, cbdesign
Printed by CPI Group (UK) Ltd, Croydon, CR0 4YY

CONTENTS

ACKNOWLEDGEMENTS

I would like to express my thanks to everyone who has contributed to this book, in particular my husband, Clive Wood, who has listened to my theories about the Holy Grail for years. Professor Sioned Davies and members of the School of Welsh at Cardiff University also acted as advisors, readers and occasional editors for various incarnations of this project, and the Centre for Lifelong Learning at Cardiff University has graciously allowed me to teach courses on various aspects of Arthurian tradition. I would also like to thank the readers for University of Wales Press for the very helpful suggestions that have helped to shape this book. Any remaining errors are of course my own. Lastly I am grateful to Sarah Lewis and Ennis Akpinar for their encouragement and patience throughout this project.

Every effort has been made to trace all copyright owners for the illustrations reproduced in this volume. The cooperation of Cardiff University Special Collections and Archives for permission to use material from their collections is gratefully acknowledged.

LIST OF
ILLUSTRATIONS

All illustrations courtesy of Cardiff University Library, Special Collections and Archives.

1. 'Perceval's Dream' from *Morte d'Arthur*, Robert Southey (ed.) (London: 1817).

2. Peredur in the Castle of Wonders from *The Mabinogion*, Charlotte Guest (tr.), 1877 edition.

3. Castell Dinas Bran and its environs, by Joseph Pennell.

4. 'Perceval on Quest' from *Sir Gawain at the Grail Castle*, Jessie Weston.

5. The West Front of Strata Florida Abbey.

6. The Nanteos Cup, J. Worthington Smith, *Archeologia Cambrensis*.

7. Welsh translations of the Prophecies of James Usher and others (1828?).

8. Manchester & Milford Railway broadside ballad, 'Taith gyda'r Railway o Benfro i Strata Florida' (n.d.).

INTRODUCTION

A LAME OLD MAN invites a young knight to his castle where he sees a maiden carrying a jewelled object called a 'graal'. This is how the writer Chrétien de Troyes introduces one of medieval literature's most enduring themes, the quest for the Holy Grail. The medieval French romance follows the adventures of the naïve and impetuous Perceval who aspires to become a worthy knight. Chrétien did not finish his romance, so we will never know exactly how he would have concluded his story. Fortunately, other medieval writers completed the grail quest. Some are known by name, some are anonymous, but they transformed Chrétien's ideas into one of the most famous episodes in Arthurian tradition. The grail became the very cup from which Jesus Christ drank at the Last Supper when he instituted the Eucharist, the sacrament by which, in medieval Christianity, ordinary bread and wine became the body and blood of Christ. By undertaking the grail quest in these romances, Arthur's knights could aspire to the supreme achievement of the code of chivalry, namely physical prowess combined with the Christian ideals of spiritual love and sacrifice.

The Arthurian connection alone makes the grail a memorable story, but continued interest in these tales led new readers to ask questions about the meaning of the romances. The attitudes of these new readers to religious history and the world of chivalry were different from those of a medieval audience, but they too wanted to identify with the grail quest and to understand the sources for the stories.

The first modern editions of the medieval grail romances appeared in the nineteenth century, and interest shifted to the origins of the grail before it was identified with King Arthur's knights and the biblical story of the Last Supper. This encouraged new speculation about the ultimate sources of the 'Grail story' and new discussions about how to interpret this mysterious object. Suggestions for the meaning of the grail include Celtic myth, ancient mystery religion, an archetypal journey, medieval heresy, occult philosophy and Templar treasure. Several relics claim to be the true grail, and they have traditions of their own. In the twentieth century, the grail story entered popular culture as a theme for biblical epics, novels, films and new religions. The search for meaning became the stuff of codes and secret documents, the centre of a vast conspiracy stretching back to the dawn of civilization. All these suggestions about the meaning of the grail share the belief that the grail story is special, something whose meaning needs to be explained.

The audiences for the first grail romances were men and women from the medieval courts of Europe. The texts reflected their concerns with personal honour, duty and a new ideal of courtly love (or *fin'amors* as modern critics prefer) between men and women. Beautiful manuscripts with lavish illustrations reflect the popularity of the tales among the wealthy. The romance stories also reflect the growing importance of lay piety and increased participation in church rituals such as the Eucharist. It was also the time of the Crusades and this heightened interest in relics and the origins of Christianity. In many ways, the romance genre reached its culmination in Thomas Malory's *Le Morte Darthur*, published by the printer, William Caxton, in 1485. Written against a background of political unrest in Britain known as the Wars of the Roses, Malory's romance coincided with an end to the feudal chivalric lifestyle and the rise of modern nation states. As a printed work, it also signalled a shift towards a wider, and less elite, audience who would read and react to narratives such as the grail story in very different ways.

In the following centuries, under the pressure of religious reformation and counter-reformation, the grail became more secular and for a time, less popular. The seventeenth century onwards witnessed the rise of Freemasonry, and its more speculative offshoots, as new networks, better adapted to the needs of a rising professional class, began to replace the aristocratic knightly orders and craftsmen's guilds. Fanciful speculations about the Crusades and the alleged symbolism of mysterious sites in Jerusalem and other parts of Europe added a layer of antiquity, romance and mystery to the newly created identities of these movements. The grail, as a biblical relic with a complex narrative heritage, was soon absorbed into this new arena and given new meaning. Another influence on ideas about the grail was the attitude of many eighteenth-century thinkers who mistrusted the old monarchies and traditional religions. To the eighteenth century, with its assumptions of rationality and progress, the European Middle Ages, encompassing roughly the fifth to fifteenth centuries, appeared to be a time of superstition and irrationality. Ironically, the conspiracy genre, which drives so much of the modern grail industry, also became prominent in this century. Fears about conspiracies were not new, but the idea that unknown forces could influence and manipulate events became more popular. Those who mistrusted the secular and modernizing tendencies of the Enlightenment created their own benevolent conspiracies that they believed guarded a 'secret wisdom' capable of restoring both social stability and the spirituality of the past. As a result groups like the Templars were, depending on one's point of view, associated with the grail story either as an evil cabal or as benevolent keepers of secret wisdom.

New editions of the medieval romances were more widely available in the nineteenth century, and this inspired new interpretations of the grail story among artists and writers who felt that the ideals of the Middle Ages could be used to reinvigorate Victorian society. Although the grail was an important theme in Victorian art and literature, it also became part of a phenomenon known as the occult revival. This transformed elements in the medieval romances into secret cults, mysterious documents and alternative forms of worship driven underground, but preserved via the hidden codes of the grail.

No matter how varied the attempts to explain and understand the grail, it is always somehow greater than any individual retelling. The factors that play a role in understanding the grail bring together medieval text, alternative history, modern fantasy, thriller novels and the infinitely varied comments on the Internet. Whether it is

Celtic folklore, archetype, ancient wisdom or alternative Christianity, it holds a key to something larger than itself. The grail has become both a realization of myth and an ever-changing contemporary legend, and since myths and legends grow out of social contexts, traditions about the Holy Grail have a complex heritage. The grail story is essentially a tale about the possession of a supernatural object, and it is this that allows it to be reinterpreted in so many imaginative ways. Many writers have speculated about the meaning of the Holy Grail legend, and their conclusions will be examined in this book. This will take us back to the 1930s and to the *fin de siècle* world of the late nineteenth and early twentieth centuries. At this time a revival of interest in the philosophies of magic and the occult melded with an interest in the origins of human culture. Beyond this is the medieval world of the grail romances themselves and the even more remote past where so many have placed the ultimate origins of this narrative.

The medieval grail was an important episode in Arthurian tradition and with the advent of mass media and the Internet, the quest for the grail now reaches an ever-wider audience. New theories about the origins of the grail have allowed writers to reinterpret it, not just as a quest motif of medieval romance, but as an image of personal and cultural transformation. Various theories about its secret meaning have adherents and detractors, and the number of books published is so vast that it would be impossible to encompass all of them. However esoteric or outlandish, these theories reflect a continued interest in the subject and the ways in which it is intertwined with contemporary popular culture. One common factor is that the Holy Grail holds a key to an esoteric world-view that, once revealed, will bring about a dramatic transformation. This adds the thrill of a detective story to the adventures of the Arthurian knights, one in which the reader can become personally involved in solving a puzzle to discover a secret. Much of this writing reflects what have come to be called 'new age' concerns about the nature of spirituality and personal development. Various commentators have addressed the truth or falsity of the ideas perpetuated by these theories; others have examined the social or psychological factors that affect people's readiness to invest in this type of knowledge. Although these were not the interests of the medieval men and women who first listened to these romances, a tale that developed in the feudal world of Western Europe has now become a myth of global proportions.

This is how the story has come down to us at the beginning of the twenty-first century. Contemporary readers are faced with a dizzying array of theories and endless possibilities. The grail quest is no longer just a theme in medieval romances aimed at a Christian audience of medieval courtiers. It now weaves in and out of modern culture and popular consciousness. What one finds in the grail castle is often a matter of individual taste, but the journey is always shaped by tradition. The question a modern Perceval might ask is not 'whom does the Grail serve?' but 'what is the Holy Grail?'

THE SOURCES OF THE GRAIL ROMANCES

T HE QUEST FOR THE GRAIL in Arthurian romance begins when the young knight, Perceval is invited by a lame nobleman to visit his castle. He witnesses a mysterious procession during dinner in which a squire enters bearing a bleeding lance followed by a beautiful girl who carries a mysterious jewelled object called *un graal*. They in turn are accompanied by candle bearers, a woman carrying an elaborate dish (called *un tailleor*) and by courtiers dressed in mourning. Perceval is too polite to enquire about this strange procession and the next day he awakes to find the castle empty. As he travels onwards, he meets a young woman who berates him for failing to ask whom the grail serves. Dispirited and confused, he begins a quest that will lead him back to the mysterious castle and to an understanding of the grail itself.

The search for the Holy Grail is one among many adventures of the knights and ladies of Arthurian tradition. These narratives, retold in the pages of medieval romance, reflect the aspirations of an aristocratic elite, the men and women who dominated the medieval world. The story of the grail and of the knights who seek it occurs in a relatively small number of romances composed during the twelfth and thirteenth centuries. The earliest account appears in a French verse-romance written about 1180 by Chrétien de Troyes. All subsequent treatments of the theme are based to some extent on this. The authors of these romances offered different explanations for the events in Chrétien's original story and introduced new themes, but the romances that followed Chrétien do not form an orderly cycle, and no consistent 'grail story' ever emerges. The idea that there was a coherent romance narrative about an object called the grail only emerged once scholars had access to modern editions of the romances.

Chrétien de Troyes composed five Arthurian romances. We know little of the author's personal history, but there are some intriguing possibilities.[1] The town of Troyes in the Champagne region of France was probably his birthplace, and some medieval scholars have detected traces of local dialect in his French. Chrétien tells us that one of his patrons gave him a book containing the story of the grail and that he based his romance on this. There is no way to know whether such a book existed. It may be the author's elegant way of acknowledging the support of a generous patron, Philip of Alsace, Count of Flanders who went on crusade in 1191 and to whom the *Story of the Grail* was dedicated. Chrétien never finished the tale. Either Philip's death on crusade or Chrétien's own death might account for why it is incomplete. What we can glean of Chrétien's life locates him in the courtly world of north-east France and Flanders in the twelfth century, but he might well have moved in similar aristocratic circles in the court of the Angevin king, Henry II of England and his queen, Eleanor of Aquitaine. Her daughter, Marie of Champagne was also Chrétien's patron, and Marie's uncle by marriage, Henry of Blois, the Anglo-Norman Abbot of Glastonbury (1101–71) was a contemporary of Geoffrey of Monmouth, Gerald of Wales and William of Malmesbury, writers who helped popularise the Arthurian legend. King Henry II had a political and personal interest in the legend of Arthur that prompted the search for Arthur's grave in the grounds of Glastonbury Abbey.

Chrétien called his poem *The Story of the Grail* (*Le conte du graal*), and it was probably composed some time between 1180 and 1190.[2] Early copyists however, often used the name of the hero, Perceval who first appears as an immature youth living in the wilds of Wales with his mother who sought refuge there after the death of her husband and other sons. His mother reluctantly watches Perceval depart to fulfil his true vocation after the boy sees knights riding through the forest and aspires to become like them. At Arthur's court a girl predicts future greatness for the lad despite taunts from the churlish Sir Kay. Perceval wins a suit of armour from a knight who has stolen Queen

Guinevere's cup and becomes squire to a nobleman who advises him on the modest behaviour expected of a knight. Eventually he sets out again to visit his mother.

After many adventures and his first love affair with the beautiful Blancheflor, he accepts hospitality from a man whom he observes fishing in a river. Thus Perceval finds himself at the grail castle, home of the Fisher King. Before dinner his crippled host presents him with a sword, which, he says, was destined for him. During the meal Perceval witnesses a strange procession in which magnificent objects are carried through the dining hall. A young man bearing a bleeding lance crosses the room followed by two more boys carrying candlesticks. A maiden carrying a jewelled object so bright that it dims the candles follows them, and mourners in turn follow her. Mindful of his mentor's advice about modest behaviour, Perceval does not ask his host about these wonders despite the fact that this procession is repeated several times during the meal. The next morning he rides away from a seemingly deserted castle, but almost immediately sees a maiden under a tree who bemoans the fact that he did not enquire about the lance or the grail. Perceval returns to Arthur's court where a loathly maiden also denounces him for failing to ask the proper question during the banquet. As a result, she tells him, the Fisher King remains in misery and his land prey to marauders. Perceval and Gawain, another important Arthurian knight, leave the security of Arthur's court to search for the grail, and they wander for a long time. On Good Friday, Perceval meets a hermit who is also his uncle. This hermit uncle explains that the Fisher King is Perceval's cousin, and that a mass-wafer from the grail miraculously sustains another king in the castle, the Fisher King's wounded father, Perceval's maternal uncle.

The grail, called *un graal* in Chrétien's romance, is not a sacred relic or even a chalice-like cup, but a large jewelled dish used for serving food, and it does not dominate the romance plot. The sword, which Perceval is given before the feast, symbolizes his development as a knight just as much as the grail, while Gawain's quest focuses on another element of the procession, the bleeding lance. The Fisher King's illness is the result of a battle wound and his land is jeopardized because the ruler is unable to defend it, not because of any magic curse. The girl sitting under the tree, whom Perceval meets when he leaves the Fisher King's castle, warns him that his sword will break at the hour of his greatest need. This and many other incidents are left unexplained in the unfinished romance. Fortunately, four subsequent romances, called *Continuations*, took up the story of Chrétien's grail. These very different attempts to complete the work transformed the grail into the sacramental object we know today.[3]

The *First Continuation*, completed before 1200 by an unknown author, concentrated on the adventures of Gawain who visits the grail castle twice. A weeping girl holds aloft 'the Holy Grail', and the bleeding lance in the procession is identified with the Lance of Longinus, the Roman centurion who pierced Christ's side at the Crucifixion. The grail procession also includes the body of a dead knight on a bier with a broken sword laid beside him, and Gawain is given an added task to mend it. On his second visit Gawain sees the grail, which provides food for everyone, floating about the hall, but he falls asleep and fails to ask the question. This romance was written only a decade after Chrétien's original, but already another writer, Robert de Boron, had transformed the object from a mysterious jewelled dish into 'The Holy Grail' and added yet another source for writers to draw on.

The author of the *Second Continuation* (1200–10), Wauchier de Danaing, shifted the focus back to Perceval. He sees candles burning in a forest and learns the next day that they are a sign of the presence of 'the rich king fisherman' and the grail. Eventually Perceval sees the lights again and enters the Fisher King's castle. Here, maidens carry both the grail and the lance and a young boy brings in the broken sword, although Perceval cannot mend it completely. New adventures that do not relate directly to the grail but reflect Perceval's growing appreciation of the ideals of knighthood were introduced into the *Continuation* texts. These include the Chapel Perilous adventures which involve battles in a mysterious cemetery and a visit to a sinister chapel whose candles are extinguished by a mysterious black hand. There is also a magic chessboard and a hunting dog and white stag which belong to Perceval's lady love and which he must retrieve before he can continue his search for the grail.

It was left to Manessier, the author of the *Third Continuation* (*c.*1210–1220) to complete the stories of Perceval and Gawain. Although the grail appears several times in this romance, the broken sword is equally important. This sword wounds the Fisher King and his brother, but after Perceval repairs it, the sword becomes the means for him to avenge his family. An angel carrying the grail heals Perceval's wounds, but only after he avenges his family does he witness the grail procession again. In this romance, the procession includes a covering for the grail, reinforcing the image of a chalice covered by its protective paten, as it would be during a Christian Mass. The Fisher King explains that the lance belonged to Longinus and the cup was used by Joseph of Arimathea to collect Christ's blood at the Crucifixion. Perceval accepts his rightful inheritance as grail king, and after ruling for seven years, he becomes a hermit. When he dies, the grail, lance, paten, and by implication the sword, go with him. The *Fourth Continuation* by Gerbert de Montreuil (*c*.1230) offers an alternative resolution to the grail romance. It takes up the story after Perceval's first failure to mend the sword. After many adventures, the knight returns to the grail castle to complete his quest. Although the attempts to finish Chrétien's narrative underline the story's popularity, they did not produce a coherent explanation for the grail.

Two thirteenth-century prologues, written in the manner of modern prequels, give additional background to the grail story. The *Bliocadran Prologue* (1200–10) narrates the history of Perceval's family.[4] His father, Bliocadran, was the last of twelve brothers. After his death in a tournament, his wife hid the infant Perceval in a forest in an effort to shield him from the dangers of knighthood's fighting code. In the *Elucidation Prologue* (1200–10) golden cups are stolen from a group of female well attendants. This is a common folktale theme about women whose lives are bound up with water sources, and the episode is linked to the loss of the Fisher King's castle. Eventually Arthur's knights avenge the maidens, Perceval and Gawain restore the grail castle and the grail floats mysteriously around the hall during a feast bringing sustenance to all.[5]

At the beginning of the thirteenth century, a Burgundian poet named Robert de Boron introduced a critical innovation to the story by identifying the grail with the cup used by Jesus Christ at the Last Supper. Like Chrétien, Robert had a crusader-patron, Gautier de Montbéliard, and he too never completed his ambitious project. Robert planned a trilogy of romances, *Joseph of Arimathea*, *Merlin* and

Perceval that would trace the history of the grail through the wanderings of St Joseph into the world of Arthur and to its conclusion in the quest undertaken by the grail knights. Only *Joseph of Arimathea* and a fragment of *Merlin* survive, but fortunately a later prose redaction, the *Roman du Graal* gives the story as Robert intended it.[6] In de Boron's version of the grail story, Pontius Pilate presented the cup that was used during the Last Supper to Joseph of Arimathea who, in turn, collected Christ's blood in it. This grail sustained Joseph in prison, and later, Joseph and his companions became the protectors of the sacred vessel. His brother-in-law, Hebron (Bron) caught a fish for a sacred feast, and at this point the Holy Grail is named specifically. It brings joy, but it also distinguishes true followers from false ones. In Robert de Boron's romance, the grail meal parallels the Last Supper story creating new links with biblical history. Eventually Joseph returns to Arimathea, while Bron becomes the Rich Fisher who journeys with the grail to Britain. Alain, one of Bron's twelve sons, also goes to Britain to await Perceval who will be keeper of the grail. In the *Merlin* romance, Arthur's magician constructs the Round Table in imitation of Joseph's grail table, which in its turn commemorated the Last Supper. Merlin also creates the Siege Perilous for the knight most worthy of the grail. All of Arthur's knights undertake the quest for the Holy Grail, and the events follow a pattern similar to Chrétien's original. Perceval fails to ask the question during his first visit to the castle of Bron, the Fisher King, and must undertake more adventures until he meets the hermit. The second time Perceval does ask the question, at which point the grail king is cured and Perceval takes his place. Eventually Merlin retires to the woods to dictate the story for posterity.[7]

The Joseph of Arimathea material derives from an Apocrypha text, a section of the *Gospel of Nicodemus* known as the *Acts of Pilate*. Although never incorporated into the Bible, the Apocrypha provided additional background to biblical events. There is no mention of a grail in the Apocrypha, only that Joseph's faith miraculously sustained him in prison, but in Robert de Boron's version, the grail is interpolated into the biblical account to create a kind of parallel Apocrypha within the romance. Even after the grail had become identified with the Last Supper and Perceval's quest completed, there remained many incidents in the story which could be further developed and elaborated, and the medieval romance genre was one in which elaboration and complex symbolism were highly regarded.

In the *Didot-Perceval* romance, composed in the second decade of the twelfth century, Perceval attempts to sit in the forbidden Siege Perilous. The grail appears, but the stone seat splits, and a voice declares a quest to lift the enchantments which Perceval's ill-advised action has caused. Although all the knights undertake this quest, only Perceval learns the secret of the Holy Grail. He asks the proper question, which cures the Fisher King and repairs the Siege Perilous, and he remains to rule the grail castle. The grail theme in this romance is set within the wider Arthurian saga, and after Perceval becomes grail king, the tale continues with Arthur's further adventures.[8]

Perlesvaus or The High Book of the Grail is a French prose romance written at the beginning of the thirteenth century.[9] The author's patron was the crusader lord, Jean de Nesle, and he too was associated with Flanders. The *Perlesvaus* romance imbued the chivalric elements drawn from Chrétien and Robert de Boron with religious and spiritual intensity. This, we are told, is the story of 'the holy vessel called the grail'. The romance opens with a lethargic Arthur uninterested in the great deeds he once performed, until Guinevere reproaches him. A maiden from the court of the Fisher King arrives during a feast, bearing the heads of knights who have died because they failed to ask the right question. Gawain makes the first, unsuccessful, attempt to accomplish the quest. He sees two maidens; one carrying the Holy Grail, the other a bleeding lance, and the grail appears as a chalice, then as a child, and finally as a crucified king. Gawain, however, is a silent witness to these events. Worse follows when Lancelot comes to the castle, as his adulterous love for the queen means that he sees nothing. In a vision, Perlesvaus's sister witnesses a spirit battle in a mysterious cemetery. She hears a voice declare that the Fisher King's evil brother, the King of Castel Mortal, has seized the Grail Castle and only the Good Knight, Perlesvaus (Perceval) can help. Once the grail, the bleeding lance and the sword of St John the Baptist are restored, King Arthur and Perlesvaus witness a procession of monks who perform the service of the Holy Grail, a service which equates the grail chalice with the Christian Eucharist. The voice speaks once more from the grail chapel and Perlesvaus boards a magic ship bound for an unknown country. This romance was the basis for a thirteenth-century Welsh adaptation, Y *Seint Greal*.[10]

The other Welsh-language romance, *Peredur fab Efrog* is one of three texts set in Arthur's court at Caerleon in Wales which are included in the medieval collection of prose tales known as *The Mabinogion*.[11] Its main theme is vengeance for the death of a kinsman. It begins where the Bliocadran prologue ends with Peredur and his mother in the forest. Although it follows the boy's awkward attempts to become a true knight and recounts the young knight's meeting with the man fishing in a river and his subsequent visit to the grail castle, the grail quest does not feature as prominently as it does in other romances. Peredur sees two young men carrying a huge spear with streams of blood flowing from it while two maidens carry a large salver with a man's bloody head. The term used to describe this object is *disgyl* (a dish) rather than grail, and Peredur later learns that the bloody head is that of his murdered cousin. When the loathly damsel berates Peredur for failing to ask questions, he learns that nine witches wounded his uncle and killed the cousin whose head is in the salver. These witches instruct Peredur in the craft of war before he takes his revenge and kills them.

The Welsh romance is not the only seemingly unusual treatment of the grail. Wolfram von Eschenbach composed a German romance, *Parzival*, in the first decade of the thirteenth century.[12] His grail is a marvellous stone called *lapsis exillis* that provides sustenance for its guardian, the grail king Anfortas. Grail knights who attend the king are called *templeise* (Templars), although they are not necessarily members of a particular order, especially since there are grail women as well. Parzival's mother is one of the women, thus the hero is related to Arthur through his father, and to the grail family through his mother. The grail king, Anfortas, although suffering from a painful groin wound, cannot die because of the presence of the grail. His virgin sister carries the grail stone, which displays a message declaring that his successor must ask a question on the first night. Many events echo earlier versions, which is not surprising since Wolfram lists Chrétien among his sources. Parzival observes the grail procession and the bleeding spear, but says nothing and is reprimanded by Cundrie, the name of the loathly maiden in this romance. He learns about his relationship to the people in the grail castle from his uncle, the hermit, as in other romances. This story is interspersed with Gawain's adventures. This maintains the contrast between the two knights and the different ways in which they embody the ideals of chivalry. In addition Parzival interacts with his pagan (i.e. part-Saracen) half-brother, Fierfiez, who is eventually baptised thereby resolving the religious contrasts as well as the contrasts of chivalry. The two brothers then travel to Munsalvaesche, the grail castle, where Parzival finally asks what ails Anfortas and becomes grail king.

Like many romance writers, Wolfram disclaimed personal responsibility for the story. In fact he claimed to be illiterate and introduced the figure of Kyout, a fictional Provençal poet, who, according to Wolfram, read an Arabic version of the grail story recorded by a Jewish astronomer in a manuscript at Toledo. This complex origin tale about lost manuscripts contrasts effectively with Wolfram's claims to be an illiterate master storyteller, but, despite attempts to substantiate the details of Wolfram's origin story, Kyout and his manuscript are undoubtedly fictions. Wolfram, like other romance writers, describes events relating to the grail, but withholds the full explanation in order to create tension and maintain suspense in the narrative. For him the 'thing called the Gral' is the stone 'lapsit exillis'. A grail family guards it at the castle of Munsalvaesche in the land of Terre de Salvaesche, and the grail king, Anfortas, has been wounded because he failed to follow the strict requirements expected of grail guardians. Only baptized Christians are able to see the grail, only a pure virgin can carry it, and only those who have been called can find the castle and its precious possession. Every Good Friday a heavenly dove renews the grail's power with a communion wafer, and from time to time messages, such as the coming of Parzival, appear on the grail stone. The sacred object provides food and drink for the inhabitants of the castle. It heals the sick and is protected by the grail king, his family and companions.

The phrase *lapsit exillis* has been explained in different ways. It may be a distortion of the Latin 'lapsis ex caelis' (that which fell from heaven) or a reference to the legend of Alexander the Great. This legend was as popular in the medieval period as the adventures of Arthur and in it, a stone from Paradise, *lapis exilis*, is sent to King Alexander to serve as a warning against pride. Such themes and references would have been relevant to the powerful Count Hermann of Thuringia who was Wolfram's patron and his knightly courtiers who made up Wolfram's main audience.

The composition of *The Lancelot Grail* (sometimes called the *Vulgate Cycle* or the *Prose Lancelot*) spans about thirty years (*c*.1215–35).[13] It transformed the grail cycle into a story about knights who go on a spiritual quest rather than one in which they have courtly adventures. The focus of the story is Lancelot, the greatest of Arthur's knights and Guinevere's lover, but it also introduced a new grail knight, Galahad. The cycle unfolds over a series of romances, two of which – *The History of the Holy Grail* (*Estoire del Saint Graal*) and the *Quest of the Holy Grail* (*Queste del Saint Graal*) – focus on the knights, Lancelot, Gawain, Perceval, Galahad and Bors. They also explain the complex and tightly knit web of relationships that link the Grail Kings and the Fisher Kings and Castle Corbennic, the home of the grail, with the city of Sarras, its ultimate destination. King Evalach of Sarras became a Christian and received a red-cross shield from Josephus. The shield is destined for a future descendant of the king's line, namely Galahad. The role of grail keeper passes from Joseph of Arimathea to his son, Josephus and to his grandson, Alain, the Rich Fisherman who guards the grail in Corbennic Castle. Pellehan, one of the guardians, is accidentally wounded in the thigh by the sword destined for Galahad, and the land becomes waste. Pellehan's son, Pelles, fathers the grail maiden Elaine, and she, in turn, becomes the mother of Galahad. When Gawain visits the grail castle, he sees the grail as a chalice carried aloft by Elaine, the future mother of Galahad. A white dove bearing a censor heralds its arrival, and everyone, except the unworthy Gawain, is served with abundant food. Lancelot's visit to the grail castle results in the conception of Galahad, and later, Lancelot's cousin, the faithful Sir Bors, sees Elaine with Lancelot's baby son. The grail heals both Bors and Perceval and eventually cures Lancelot's madness. Despite the emphasis on the Christian and Eucharistic qualities of the grail in the *Vulgate Cycle*, it is still carried by a maiden in the grail procession and retains its healing and nourishing qualities.

In the *Queste del Saint Graal*, Galahad occupies the Siege Perilous and receives the red-cross shield. The appearance of the Holy Grail is attended by sweet odours and plentiful food and heralds the commencement of the quest. This quest follows the familiar romance format of adventures in dark forests, voyages to mysterious castles and encounters with the grail at Corbennic and Sarras. In a crucial scene in the romance, Joseph of Arimathea's son, Josephus, celebrates the grail mass whose symbolism resolves some of the details of earlier grail processions. Here for example, the blood from the lance runs into the grail, and the knights experience visions that include images of the Trinity, a child and the figure of the wounded Christ rising from the grail vessel. This is in effect a symbolic vision of the theological doctrine of the Eucharist in which water and wine were miraculously transformed into the body and blood of Christ. Worldly knights like Gawain are ultimately excluded, and Lancelot, although a repentant sinner, is granted only a partial vision. Both Bors and Perceval experience the grail in its Eucharistic aspect, but only Galahad achieves a final vision of the Holy Grail at Sarras. Once this is accomplished, a mysterious hand appears and removes the grail, its ornamental covering and the lance forever.

Heinrich von dem Türlin's romance, *The Crown* (*Diu Crône*), dates from about 1240. The form of the grail in this romance, a reliquary containing bread, reflects the changing rituals surrounding the Eucharist service, in this instance, one in which the consecrated bread was shown to lay believers outside the context of the Mass. The author's extensive list of sources reflects the popularity of the grail romances in the medieval period, but Gawain is the main hero, and the grail quest is one among many adventures.[14] Gawain's journey to the grail castle resembles a traditional wonder tale. He receives help from a magician's sister who later carries the grail. At the grail castle, Lancelot is drugged with magic wine, but Gawain, who has been forewarned, witnesses an elaborate grail procession during a wondrous feast. Two girls carry candlesticks, two boys carry a spear from which fall three drops of blood, two more girls hold an ornate bowl, and a lady enters with a reliquary containing bread. A weeping woman attends the procession, and the lord of the castle explains that although this is the grail, Perceval's failure means that they, in effect a company of the living dead, will disappear forever.

Shropshire is the setting for a romance about an outlaw hero, *Foulk fitz Warin* (*c*.1250), which includes a grail episode probably influenced by *Perlesvaus*.[15] The late thirteenth-century metrical romance, *Sone de Nansai* locates the story of Joseph of Arimathea and the grail castle in Norway, but in other respects it is peripheral to the grail story.[16] The *Prose Tristran* (*c*.1250) draws together several significant Arthurian knights on a grail quest. Galahad mends the broken sword and cures his grandfather, Palamedes, by rubbing blood from the Lance on his legs and thighs. At the end of the romance, Galahad, Perceval and Bors carry the grail onto a ship and sail to Sarras.[17] One of the last in the group of texts which came to be called the grail romances is the mid- thirteenth century *Roman du Graal* (or the Post-Vulgate Cycle). In it, a knight called Balin unwittingly uses a holy lance to wound King Pellehan. This episode is known as the Dolorous Stroke and it explains how the Maimed King (or Fisher King) was wounded and came to rule over the Wasteland.

Sir Thomas Malory's *Le Morte Darthur* is perhaps the greatest version of the Arthurian legend in English. William Caxton's edition introduced the world of knightly deeds to a new, less courtly, audience, and Malory was the departure point for the revival of the Arthurian legend in Britain and elsewhere in the nineteenth century. Details about his life, like those of so many other romance authors who have written about the grail, are surprisingly elusive. Sir Thomas Malory of Newbold Revel was born into an English gentry family in 1405. He was active in public life, but his career was far from smooth. From certain references in the romance supported by other documents, he evidently composed *Le Morte Darthur* while in prison. He died in 1471 and his life was played out against the background of the dynastic struggles that culminated in the Wars of the Roses and resulted in the emergence of a dramatically changed Britain under the Tudors. This adds poignancy to his tales of chivalry composed as they were at such an important cultural turning point. Malory distilled the whole of his extensive knowledge of Arthurian romance into *Le Morte Darthur*, which was completed by 1470 and published by William Caxton in 1485. The sections dealing with grail material include the episode of Balin and the Dolorous Stroke, the story of Lancelot and Elaine and the conception of Galahad, and finally 'The noble tale of the Sankreall which is called the holy vessel and the signification of blessed blood of Our Lord Jesu Christ, which was brought into this land by Joseph of Arimathea.'[18]

Malory drew on earlier sources, in particular the *Lancelot-Grail* and *Post Vulgate* material. He reshaped them in a way that resolved some of the conflicting details about the grail quest. According to *Le Morte Darthur*, Pellam, the Fisher King, was wounded by Balin's Dolorous Stroke and could only be healed by Galahad. This frames the tale and links the origin of the Fisher King's wound with Galahad's ultimate success. In *The Tale of the Sankegreal*, as Malory tells it, Lancelot sees the grail at Corbennic Castle and it is here that Elaine, the daughter of the grail keeper Pelles, conceives Galahad. Bors and Perceval also have visions of the grail at Corbennic, but only Galahad sees the full 'marvels of the Sankgreall'. Malory focuses on the grail as the vessel in which Christ's blood was collected on the Cross. This certainly reflected the belief that the grail was the Christian Eucharist cup that contained Christ's blood during the Mass, but it may also reflect Malory's personal knowledge of the Holy Blood relic preserved at Hailes Abbey in England during his lifetime.[19]

A few details relevant to the grail narrative are to be found in other romances. For example, Henry Lovelich's *The History of the Holy Grail* is roughly contemporary with Malory's work. Lovelich stressed Merlin's role as prophet of the Holy Grail and added the important detail that Joseph of Arimathea was buried at Glastonbury. John Hardyng, another contemporary of Malory, defended Arthur's reputation as a real British hero against historians who were beginning to question his reality. Hardyng interpreted *san greal*, 'holy grail', as *sang real*, 'royal blood'. In this version Galahad finds the grail in Wales and establishes an order of *Sanke Roiall* in Palestine to fight against the Saracens. Perceval brings Galahad's red-cross shield back to Glastonbury where Galahad's heart is eventually buried.[20]

Despite the vast antiquity often attributed to the grail and later the Holy Grail, its appearance in literary form occurred within a single century. During this time it developed from a mysterious jewelled object into a sacred relic of the Eucharist which could heal both physically and spiritually. In so far as the grail had a meaning for medieval readers, it fulfilled the expectations of educated courtly and religious elites. During the sixteenth century, in the immediate aftermath of the Reformation, references to the grail began to decline and no new grail romances were written. The religious significance of the grail begins to weaken and the knights become less relevant to the quest. The fact that no consistent 'grail story' emerges from the romances is undoubtedly one of the factors that opened the way for modern speculations about the origin and meaning for the grail after interest began to revive in the nineteenth century. Nevertheless, the universal appeal of the grail story was to prove surprisingly robust in the years ahead.

THE CHARACTERS
IN THE GRAIL QUEST

THE ROMANCE PLOT, in which heroes undertake quests and true lovers triumph through adversity, seems so familiar that it is almost a cliché. However at the beginning of the twelfth century, it was a relatively new genre bound by a distinct set of rules and conventions, centred on a hero who underwent tests and adventures in pursuit of a goal. The French verse narratives of Chrétien de Troyes introduced the idea of courtly love or *fin'amors* in which a chivalrous and heroic knight undertook these adventures and tribulations to win the love of a lady. Often the main character's actions were part of a quest in which the adventures became subordinate to this overriding goal. Prose rather than verse romances became popular in the thirteenth century and with them a new fashion for cycles with even more intricate plots in which the adventures of several knights were interwoven. This structure was well suited to the Holy Grail story and finding the grail was often closely linked with winning a wife. The grail romances were also part of a wider thematic cycle, the 'Matter of Britain' or tales about the deeds of King Arthur and his knights. Chrétien de Troyes's romance combined these elements. It was not only the first literary realization of the grail story, but it integrated this theme into the world of chivalry. Chrétien presented the grail as a means to examine the nature of the chivalric ideal in relation to courage, but also in relation to love and to spirituality. Whatever alterations subsequent authors made to the story, this core remained.

THE KNIGHTS OF THE GRAIL

Five knights search for the grail in medieval romance, Perceval, Gawain, Lancelot, Bors and Galahad. In the earlier romances based closely on Chrétien's original story and its *Continuations*, Perceval and Gawain undertake the grail quest. In the later romances, especially the *Vulgate Cycle* or the *Lancelot-Grail* as it is also called, the focus shifts to Lancelot and eventually to his son Galahad. Lancelot's cousin, Sir Bors provides a link between the earlier quest knights, Perceval and Gawain and the later father/son pairing of Lancelot and Galahad. Bors also fulfils the important role of overall narrator when the grail quest is finally completed. Sir Thomas Malory attempted to integrate this material into *Le Morte Darthur* in the fifteenth century, but even then, a truly consistent narrative does not emerge. This is undoubtedly one factor that produces such a wide range of interpretations of the grail and its meaning. Modern readers have the luxury of being able to read all the sources for the medieval grail romances and can gain a better perspective on how characters and situations develop, but even now many details remain obscure and unexplained.

Perceval (also called Peredur, Parzival and Perlesvaus) is the first grail knight to appear. He is an eager but awkward youth struggling to find an identity, and when he meets the knights in the forest, he abandons his mother to seek his fortune. At Arthur's court, he wins a suit of armour from a marauding knight. This is only the outward symbol of knighthood, and a kindly knight teaches him the rudiments of chivalry. Even then the limitations of his understanding and insight become clear at the court of the Fisher King when he fails to ask the proper question about the grail. When this failure is highlighted by the girl sitting under a tree and later by the loathly damsel, a chastened Perceval sets out again. After many adventures, which test his fitness to be a knight, he meets a hermit and finally understands the true meaning of chivalry. He then returns to the castle of the wounded king, asks the proper question and assumes the role of grail king.

The *Fourth Continuation* developed Perceval's character further. In this version, he almost mends the sword, except for a little notch that signifies that Perceval has not yet repented for his treatment of his mother and not yet achieved the ideal of knighthood. Perceval's role continued to be important in the romances that completed Chrétien's tale and he is the central figure in Wolfram's von Eschenbach's *Parzival*, the Welsh *Peredur* and the French *Perlesvaus*. While he develops somewhat differently in these romances, the events in Chrétien's original unfinished romance provide the key to his character.

Family and the discovery of identity are important facets in Perceval's development. The young man is initially unaware of his identity in a world bounded by the wilderness and his mother. In Chrétien's story, Perceval's two brothers have been killed in tournaments and his father has died of grief. In the alternative account in *The Bliocadran Prologue*, Perceval's father, Bliocadran, and his eleven brothers are all killed in tournaments. In *The Bliocadran Prologue* the emphasis falls on the dangers of the chivalric lifestyle, while in Chrétien's story the deaths of Perceval's brothers cause his father's death. This situation parallels the fate of Perceval's mother who also dies of grief after her son's departure, and this is one of the reasons for Perceval's troubles. He leaves his mother with hardly a backward glance once he meets the knights. After his first visit to the Grail castle, he sees a girl under a tree weeping over a dead knight. She is his cousin, and when he admits that he did not ask about the lance or the grail, she warns him that his sword will break in his hour of need and asks him his name. Finally, despite his failure at the Fisher King's castle, he knows who he is. He makes amends for his previous impulsive behaviour, but his return to Arthur's court is marred by the appearance of a loathly damsel who tells him that his mother has died of grief, and, because of his failure, the Fisher King's wounds will not heal. Perceval wanders, never resting two nights in the same place and never going to church. Finally, on Good Friday, he arrives at the cell of another relative, a hermit uncle, who informs Perceval that his troubles are the result of his actions towards his mother. He also tells his nephew that the grail castle contains two kings, both relatives of the young knight, and that the grail sustains the older king who needs no other food.

In the *Didot-Perceval*, Perceval has a different family history. He is the son of Alain le Gros, and therefore part of the family of Joseph of Arimathea and Bron, the original Fisher/Grail king. In Wolfram's *Parzival* his father is Gamuret who had a son by a pagan woman, the brother whom Parzival fights unknowingly and then converts to

Christianity. Parzival's own mother Herzeloyde, is one of the grail guardians. This links Perceval to the grail family as well as to Arthur. The details of his heritage vary, but the effect is the same. Perceval's mother decides to raise her son in the wilderness where he will be safe from the dangers of chivalry's warrior ethos and his quest is to find himself in finding the grail.

As the romances became more elaborate, Perceval undertook further adventures. Some concerned his ladylove, since love of family, love of one's lady and the love of God were intertwined in the world of courtly romance. One important adventure, which is very much in the tradition of courtly love romances, concerns a stag head and a hunting hound given to him by a woman. He loses these objects and has to recapture them before he can finish his grail adventure.

In the Welsh romance *Peredur*, family and vengeance dominate the role of grail hero and even supersede the search for the grail. Peredur begins as a naïve and impetuous youth as in other grail romances. The untutored boy is strong and adventurous, swift enough to herd wild animals among domesticated ones, but too ignorant to know the difference. Inevitably he meets some knights and leaves his mother's care. She gives him some advice which, in his bumptious naivety, he takes too literally. He arrives at Arthur's court where he is both praised and taunted. He kills a rogue knight and clothes himself in the armour of his defeated foe, thus taking on the appearance at least of knighthood. Like a typical romance hero, Peredur embarks on a series of adventures. He visits the castle of an unknown uncle who advises him on knightly restraint. Just as the impulsive Peredur followed his mother's advice too literally, he reacts to his uncle's advice too carefully. He meets a man fishing by a lake and dines with him in a castle. With his immense strength and knightly potential, Peredur strikes his sword against an iron column. When the sword fails to repair itself on the third stroke, his uncle declares that Peredur has not yet acquired his full strength. At the second castle, he sees a bleeding lance and a head in a bloody platter, but he fails to ask about them. Next day Peredur's foster-sister berates him for his silence and explains that his relatives have been wounded by the witches of Caerloyw (Gloucester). These witches teach him fighting skills. Eventually he returns to Arthur's court, but sets out again on a hunt which leads to further adventures full of marvels, noxious beasts, a magic chess game, various supernatural opponents, and a beautiful woman, the Empress of Constantinople. One version of the Peredur tale ends at this point, but a second variant has further adventures. These bring him back to the Castle of Wonders, where the meaning of the mysterious procession is explained to the young hero who is now a worthy knight. The head belonged to his cousin, murdered by the witches of Caerloyw, and the tale concludes with the defeat of the witches.

The grail romances develop three aspects of Perceval's character, his links to his family, his love for a lady, and his understanding of the true spiritual meaning of the grail. The innate sophistication of the second grail knight, Gawain is the perfect foil for Perceval's growth from awkward boy into true knight. In the context of the grail romances, Gawain's search for the bleeding lance parallels Perceval's grail adventure. He too is related to Joseph of Arimathea, and like Perceval, linked by ties of blood to the grail family. Gawain undergoes his own series of adventures. One of the most striking takes place in a mysterious chapel where a sinister Black Hand snuffs out the candles. Both knights fail to ask the correct question on their first visit to the grail castle, but both have the opportunity to make amends. The adventures of these two characters are frequently entwined in grail romances in a way that contrasts the courtly, but worldly, chivalry embodied in Gawain with the idealistic and ultimately more spiritual chivalry achieved by Perceval.

As Arthur's nephew, Gawain is one of the most important Knights of the Round Table, and his adventures extend beyond the grail quest. His character varies considerably in different romances, but he is always courteous and as attracted to women and they are to him. Gawain's behaviour towards Perceval when the latter contemplates the blood-spotted snow, a reminder of his mistress's beauty, marks him out as the most courteous knight. This quality endears him to women when, for example, he frees an entire castle full of captives among whom are his own relatives. However, this essentially worldly courtesy prevents him from full achievement of the grail quest. He provides a contrast to Perceval's more idealistic chivalry and when the relationships among the grail knights change with the introduction of Lancelot, Bors and Galahad, Gawain's role diminishes. In the

Lancelot Grail romances, Galahad became the perfect Grail knight, while Gawain's character became distracted by women and worldly concerns, and in Malory's *Le Morte Darthur*, his position becomes that of the knight who failed the grail quest.

Another knight, Sir Bors (also called Bohort) is introduced into the thirteenth-century *Lancelot Grail* cycle. He is Lancelot's cousin who acts as companion to the other grail knights and eventually returns to Arthur's court to recount the conclusion of the grail adventures. The ever-faithful Bors is the third knight to witness the Holy Grail at Castle Corbennic where, on a later visit, he also sees the infant Galahad. He accompanies Perceval and Galahad on the mysterious ship built by King Solomon, which takes them to Sarras, the city of the grail. After Perceval and Galahad have witnessed the grail, Bors returns to Arthur's court. He is however, more than just an observer or the survivor who tells the story. He undergoes a bizarre series of adventures at the Palace of Adventures where he is wounded by a flaming lance and fights with a knight who uses the grail to renew his strength. Bors recognises the power of the grail and eventually sees it in all its glory.

Lancelot is the knight closest to Arthur and would seem to be the most appropriate one to find the grail. However, as the grail quest became more spiritual, Lancelot's adultery with Guinevere clashed with his ability to achieve the quest. Towards the end of the *Lancelot Grail*, the knight observes the grail on a silver table behind a locked grill in a small chapel. Lancelot falls asleep and is unaware of a passing knight who is cured by the grail and asks his companion about the sleeper only to be told that this is a knight who has committed some sin, which will prevent him achieving the quest of the grail. As so often in medieval romance this prediction is fulfilled when Lancelot visits Castle Corbennic. He sees a priest celebrating mass with the grail. When he approaches too closely, he is struck down, but the power of the grail cures his madness. Malory's portrait of Lancelot in *Le Morte Darthur* is perhaps the most sympathetic. He portrays him as a knight who strives for perfection and in the section that Caxton entitled 'The Tale of the Sangreal', although Galahad achieves the final vision, Lancelot does share the action with the other grail knights.

The ultimate grail knight is Galahad. In later romances like the *Lancelot Grail* and Malory, he replaces Perceval to a great extent. As the son of Lancelot and a grail maiden, Elaine, who is a daughter of the Fisher King, he occupies the Siege Perilous, the place at the Round Table destined for the one who will find the grail. Through his mother Elaine and his grandfather Pelles who is the wounded king, Galahad's heritage goes back to Joseph of Arimathea and the original grail guardians. He is also connected to the Old Testament warrior kings who were much admired in the world of medieval chivalry. To emphasize this heritage, Galahad finds and carries the sword of King David, which had been placed on Solomon's ship, the vessel that takes the worthy grail knights to Sarras. He also receives the shield of Evalach, king of the grail kingdom of Sarras, who was converted by Josephus, the son of Joseph of Arimathea. Josephus inscribed this shield with a red cross made from his own blood. This complex network of associations, which for many modern readers slows down the action of the romances, emphasized the religious meaning of the grail by creating links between Old and New Testament figures. As these biblical figures were also warriors and kings, they were important symbols of medieval nobility and prowess as well.

Galahad's appearance at the beginning of the *Queste del Graal* (part of the *Lancelot Grail*) is in marked contrast with Perceval's gauche naiveté. Galahad's coming to Camelot is preceded by portents. These include a message written on the Siege Perilous as if by magic, the appearance of a sword embedded in a floating stone and prophesies uttered by Merlin. Galahad occupies the Siege Perilous and draws the sword where other knights have failed. This signals the appearance of the Holy Grail floating above the Round Table at Arthur's court, accompanied by a sweet odour and dispensing food for all. The time appropriately is the Feast of Pentecost, when the Holy Spirit descended on the followers of Christ and this provides yet another parallel between Galahad's quest and biblical events.

The five grail knights embody different aspects of chivalry. Gawain's earthly ideals contrast with Perceval, the gauche boy who attains true knighthood and eventually succeeds the lord of the grail castle. Bors is faithful to his quest and returns to Arthur's court. Lancelot is the bravest with his unshakable courtly devotion to his lady Guinevere, and Galahad embodies the total spiritual transformation of the chivalric code. Arthur is not a grail knight, but as king he provides a symbolic centre for the grail quest, and his role embodies some of the ambiguities of that quest. Arthur presides over the Round Table. After Merlin introduces Galahad as the occupant of the Siege Perilous, it is King Arthur who sanctions the departure of the knights on their quest for the Holy Grail. However at the beginning of *Perlesvaus*, the king is listless both physically and spiritually until Guinevere sends him off searching for Perceval. Arthur later witnesses the mass of the Grail, and finally Bors returns to Camelot, to tell Arthur the conclusion of the grail quest.

THE WOMEN OF THE GRAIL ROMANCES

Although the knights take the most active roles in medieval romance, women are nonetheless important. According to the demands of courtly love or *fin'amors*, knights needed to be brave warriors, but they also were also required to display courtesy towards women, and this was expressed in terms of love and devotion directed towards one particular woman. This love ranged from the very real sexual attraction between Lancelot and Guinevere, to Gawain's multiple liaisons and Perceval's striving to obtain the hand of his beloved in marriage. It also included the intense otherworldly spirituality of Galahad, and to some extent that of Sir Bors, which was not directed to earthly love, but to the idea of *caritas*, the Christian ideal of love. Even after the grail story moved the quest into a more spiritual realm, the role of women remained significant.

The central female role is the grail bearer. In one sense this seems odd once the grail became identified with the cup of the Last Supper and the Eucharist, since women did not participate actively in the celebration of the Christian mass, but as women embodied the dynamic between *amor* and *caritas* in the courtly love code, they complement the achievements of the grail knights.

On most occasions in the romances, a beautiful maiden carries the grail, and the role of female grail-bearer remains constant, quite possibly because the romances were not devotional works and there was therefore no conflict with religious practice. Women were however an indispensable part of the courtly quest and a female grail-bearer further underlined the fusion between courtly and spiritual chivalry. Occasionally the grail maiden is named; in *Parzival*, she is Repanse de Shoye, and in the later *Vulgate Cycle* romances, the grail maiden becomes the mother of Galahad. Lancelot is tricked into sleeping with Elaine of Corbennic after he rescues her. This ruse provides Lancelot with a son, Galahad, who will be the perfect knight, while allowing Lancelot himself to remain faithful to Guinevere in the true spirit of *fin'amors*. As part of the line of Joseph of Arimathea, Elaine confers this distinctive heritage on Galahad. However once she has taken a lover, she can no longer be the bearer of the grail, and when Bors visits the castle she has passed on the role of grail maiden to her cousin.

In several of the grail romances, Perceval falls in love with a beautiful woman, whom he eventually marries. She is called Blancheflor by Chrétien and Condwiramurs by Wolfram. In the Welsh *Peredur*, he falls in love with an otherworld lady called the Empress of Constantinople. He accomplishes a series of tasks to win her hand and he reigns with her for a time before continuing on his quest to avenge his family and understand the meaning of the grail procession.

Perceval's relations with women reflect more than just the prowess and courtesy expected of knights in medieval romance. They also demonstrate that emotional maturity is just as important in the grail quest as his ability to perform daring and difficult feats. At the beginning of the romances in which Perceval is a major character, he is living in the wilderness with his mother. In medieval romance the wilderness contrasts with the civilized world of Arthur's court. It is an enigmatic landscape, a place for adventure and an opportunity for the knights to prove themselves. For Perceval, the opposition between the wilderness and the civilized world has a particular meaning. Unlike the other knights who move from court to wilderness, Perceval begins by knowing nothing of the court or indeed male society but only the wilderness. He leaves without any thought to his mother's pain at losing the last male member of her family. He treats a noble woman in a tent in accordance with a literal interpretation of his mother's advice, but in a manner far from consistent with the demands of chivalry. Later after he has matured, he makes restitution to this lady, but at the beginning of the romance his boorish behaviour towards both mother and lady indicates just how far Perceval must travel. At

Arthur's court, a girl who has never laughed prophesies that Perceval will become a great knight and is rebuffed by the discourteous Sir Kay. Perceval later avenges this insult, but it is not until he meets the Lady Blanchflor that the ennobling quality of love begins to change the brash young knight. In a subsequent scene, repeated in many of the grail romances, Perceval contemplates drops of red blood from a falcon's prey, which have fallen on the white snow. The colours recall the beauty of his mistress and they distract him, although not so completely that he cannot unhorse two knights who approach him. Finally the courteous Gawain rouses him from his reverie. This not only establishes that Perceval has begun to act like a courtly lover, but it introduces the friendship between Perceval and Gawain.

The explanation for the significance of the mysterious adventures undertaken by the knights is often delayed. This is a common device used to build suspense and to move the plot forward. In the grail romances women and hermits often provide these explanations, but their function is not just an opportunity for some necessary plot explanation. After Perceval's initial visit to the grail castle in Chrétien's romance, he meets a lady weeping over a dead knight. She asks him whether he enquired about the grail and the lance, and when he admits that he did not, she predicts disaster and warns him that his new sword will shatter. The lady is his cousin who also berates him about his inconsiderate behaviour to his mother, making it clear that Perceval has not yet understood what is required of a knight and a grail seeker. In *Parzival*, this lady is given a name, Sigune, and the tragic history of her love for the dead knight is revealed. After Perceval returns to Arthur's court, the loathly damsel, called Cundrie in Wolfram's romance, appears and also berates his failure. This is a turning point for Perceval who rushes from Arthur's court back into the wilderness vowing never to rest or to enter a church. This in effect isolates him from the civilized world of courtly society and the comfort of religion as surely as his childhood in the wilderness. Eventually these conflicts are resolved and Perceval asks the question which cures the King. Thus he achieves his destiny to become grail king and he marries his lady.

Perceval's sister appears in the later grail romances. She foresees coming events such as the terrible vision in the Perilous Cemetery where she beholds the temporary loss of the grail castle to a demonic king. As the central importance of Perceval's role as grail seeker altered with the addition of other knights, especially Galahad, Perceval's sister became more fully integrated into the elaborate symbolic network that linked the biblical world in which the grail first appeared with the Arthurian world where it will be found. In the *Vulgate* and *Le Morte Darthur*, she leads Galahad to Solomon's ship and then uses her own hair to weave a new sword belt for the one left by Solomon's wife. Her actions emphasise the theme that the new Christian world replaces the old. In Malory, she offers a basin filled with her own blood to cure the Leprous Lady of a disease which often symbolised the sinfulness of humanity as a whole. This sacrifice brings about her own death, and ultimately, Perceval's sister is the female character who comes closest to a human embodiment of the grail.

Guinevere is of course the woman who causes Lancelot to stray from the grail quest, but she remains the focus of Lancelot's devotion despite the attempts of the fairy queens to seduce him and the fact that he fathers his only son, Galahad, with another woman. Although Guinevere is somewhat less important than other female figures in the grail story, she takes an active role in the *Perlesvaus* romance where she berates Arthur for his listlessness and causes him to go on quest with his knights.

HERMITS AND PROPHETS

In many grail romances Perceval makes a Good Friday visit to a hermit who is also his uncle. Wolfram calls him Trevrizont, but often he is unnamed. This hermit uncle unites several strands in the grail romance structure. He reveals the importance of Perceval's spiritual nature and the need for him to understand his mother's grief. He also imparts information about his most important relative, the grail king, whose role Perceval will eventually inherit, as the fulfilment of his destiny of which he was ignorant at the beginning of his quest. In one romance, Perceval himself becomes a hermit, thereby completing the spiritual as well as the family theme. Bringing such themes full circle is an important feature of the romance technique.

The figure of Merlin became absorbed into the grail stories through Robert de Boron's romance *Merlin* and in sections of the *Vulgate Cycle*. As a prophet of the grail, his role is comparable to that of the hermits. He constructs the Round Table as a deliberate echo of Joseph of Arimathea's grail table, which in turn commemorated the original Passover feast. He helps Perceval in his search for the grail and introduces Galahad as the rightful occupant of the Siege Perilous. Eventually Merlin retires to dictate the story of the grail quest and becomes a kind of hermit himself.

THE GRAIL CASTLE AND FISHER KING

The grail appears as a mysterious floating entity at Arthurian feasts, but it is also kept in an equally mysterious castle presided over by a wounded king and his entourage. The castle is not always named, but sources such as the *Vulgate Cycle* and Malory locate it at a place called Corbennic (Corbenic, Carbonek, Carbonic). Where Perceval is the central character, he eventually returns to this castle to ask the right question and to take up his role as grail king. Galahad is also closely connected with the location and can trace his lineage back to the original grail guardians and the grail castle. Alain le Gros, son of Bron the Rich Fisher and a member of St Joseph's family, visits a leprous king who is cured by the grail. This king builds a castle to house the sacred object. His descendant, Pelles is lord of Corbennic, father of Elaine the grail bearer and Galahad's grandfather.

Sarras is the name of the castle to which the knights carry the Holy Grail. Its ruler was King Evalach who became a Christian and whose shield is destined for Galahad. After the three knights Bors, Perceval and Galahad accompany the grail to Sarras, Galahad reigns as king for a year, followed by Perceval. After the latter's death, Bors returns to Arthur's court. In *Peredur* the grail castle is called the Castle of Wonders and this is where Peredur sees the head of his dead cousin whom he must avenge. Wolfram's names for the grail castle and its location reflect the idea of salvation. Munsalvaesche (Monsalvat) is located in the mysterious Terre de Salvache. The castle can only be found by chosen Christian knights and is protected by King Anfortas and the grail guardians. In Wolfram's romance, the grail king, Anfortas, is Parzival's uncle who suffers because he did not fulfil the strict code expected of Wolfram's grail knights. Specifically he allowed his courtesy towards women to outweigh his devotion to the grail by taking a wife in violation of the requirements of the grail guardians. Although courtesy is a central tenet of the chivalric code, spiritual devotion becomes a higher virtue in the grail romances.

Sometimes the grail king is unnamed. The earliest grail romance has two kings, both of whom are related to Perceval. One of them, Le Roi Pecheur, meets Perceval while he is fishing and invites the young knight to the castle, and the other is wounded and sustained by the host from the *graal*. Robert de Boron's romance trilogy gives more details about this pivotal figure. Before the grail was taken to Britain, Hebron (Bron), the brother-in-law of Joseph of Arimathea, caught a fish and placed it on the grail table. He became known as the Rich Fisher and is by extension the Fisher King when he becomes lord of the grail castle in Britain. His son, Alain is also called a Fisher King. In the *Lancelot Grail Cycle*, Josephus grants guardianship of the grail to Alain le Gros, Bron's twelfth son, who is called the Rich Fisherman because the fish he catches mysteriously multiply. In the *Perlesvaus* romance he is also Perceval's father. Anfortas, the grail king in Wolfram, suffers because he fought for a woman not the grail alone, and the expected question is different, not 'Whom does the grail serve?' but 'Why do you suffer so?' King Pelles is called the Maimed King because he drew the sword on Solomon's ship and wounded himself through the thighs. His son is either wounded in battle or unwittingly wounded with Longinus's spear by the tragic Balin. In a somewhat unusual version of the grail story the *Sone de Nausai*, Joseph of Arimathea is the Fisher King.

Usually the Fisher King and Grail King are separate characters, but sometimes they are identical. The Fisher/Grail King is often wounded or sick. His sickness is sometimes reflected in the state of his kingdom, which has become a wasteland, although this is not always the case. However he can only be healed when the preordained visitor to his castle asks the proper question; 'Whom does the grail serve?'

THE FAMILY OF JOSEPH OF ARIMATHEA AND SOLOMON'S SHIP

Legends from the fifteenth century onwards stress Joseph's role as a saint who brought Christianity to Britain and Glastonbury, but Joseph is first linked specifically with the grail in Robert de Boron's twelfth-century romance. Here, and in the *Perlesvaus*, he is called *decurio*, that is a soldier and, therefore, a suitable patron for the grail knights and the courtly and military audience who first read these romances. In the grail romances, Pontius Pilate gives Joseph of Arimathea the cup used at the Last Supper which Joseph uses to collect the blood flowing from Christ's wounds on the cross and again from his wounds before he is buried. Josephus, son of Joseph of Arimathea according to the thirteenth-century *Vulgate*, becomes the first bishop who miraculously transports his followers over the sea on his tunic to bring the grail to Britain. Before his death Josephus inscribes a red cross in his own blood on a shield given to King Avalach (Evalach). This shield remained at Glastonbury until Galahad claimed it. Bron (Hebron) is Joseph's brother-in law who catches a fish for the first grail table and becomes known as the 'rich fisher' and his son, Alain, inherits the roles of Fisher and Grail King. As a descendant of Alain, Perceval is closely associated with the grail and its guardians.

The introduction of a fictional Apocrypha story about Joseph and the Holy Grail into Robert de Boron's romances created new links between the grail romances and the biblical past. Medieval authors rose to this challenge with beautiful and complex images and new episodes which demonstrate their ability to expand traditional themes. Mysterious ships are common enough in traditional literature, but in the later grail romances, the ship which takes the grail heroes to their destination is associated with important Old Testament figures like Solomon and David, and it becomes infused with new layers of symbolism. Like the Joseph story, Solomon's ship links the Bible and the grail knights, although here the connections are with the Old Testament warrior kings rather than New Testament figures. Like Solomon's Temple, the materials from which the ship is made are symbolic of eternity and constancy. Objects on board the ship, like the sword of the warrior-king, David, are destined for the grail knights. The bed is decorated with spindles from the Tree of Life, and when Perceval's sister weaves a new belt for King David's sword using her own hair, the knights are drawn into the network of female figures starting with Eve extending to the Blessed Virgin and including the grail women as well.

THE GRAIL PROCESSION

This brings us to the object of the quest, the grail itself. The Latin word, *gradale*, refers to a wide, flat serving plate, rather than a chalice or cup. This is often pointed out in discussions that look for a pre-Christian meaning for the grail, although it is not clear how common this term was before the grail romances were written. According to Chrétien, the object called *un graal* is a jewelled sacred thing, but not clearly a chalice or mass cup. Robert de Boron calls it the Holy Grail and connects it to the Last Supper story through the apocryphal account of Joseph of Arimathea. The *Continuations* completed Chrétien's tale and were influenced by de Boron as well. As a result, the grail became identified with the Eucharist cup, and later romances, for example the *Lancelot Grail*, elaborated this religious symbolism further. The knights see not just the grail, but multiple visions of Christ, first as a child, then crucified on the cross and finally triumphantly transformed. Sometimes a dove, the symbol of the Holy Spirit, accompanies the grail. Wolfram departs from this imagery, although not radically. The grail is a stone to which a dove brings a mass wafer to reinvigorate it every year. In later German versions the grail is identified with a jewel from the crown of the fallen angel, Lucifer, which emphasises the notion of redemption and salvation. In some romance traditions it is also the platter from which Christ and the apostles ate the Pascal lamb at the Last Supper, recalling here the idea of sacrifice. The grail's form ranges from a plain round bowl to an elaborate reliquary containing bread like those used in church services. The illustrations to medieval romances, some of which depict the grail as a chalice, as a plain bowl, and as jewelled object emitting light, reflect this diversity as well.

The account of the Dolorous Blow in later romances provides an explanation of how the Fisher King received his wound and reflects the shift to Galahad as the ultimate grail seeker. Pellam (Pellehan) is one of the wounded kings who await the grail knight. In the thirteenth-century *Vulgate Estoire*, Pellehan received an incurable wound in a battle at Rome. However in an episode in the Post-Vulgate *Suite de Merlin* which was later expanded by Malory, the Dolorous Stroke, or Dolorous Blow, was delivered by the knight Balin in his quest for vengeance. Balin mistakenly uses the Spear of Longinus to inflict an injury on King Pellam, thereby becoming the cause of the grail king's incurable wound. Sometimes this wound transforms Pellam's kingdom into a wasteland. According to Malory only Galahad can heal him. In a further tragic development Balin keeps a sword, despite the warning that it is cursed, and unwittingly kills his own brother. This sword is later drawn from a floating stone by Galahad.

Other objects in the grail procession are also important. Perceval, Gawain and Galahad are all associated with swords. In the earliest grail romance Perceval is given the sword before he sees the grail procession, and is told that in order to repair this sword he must prove himself a worthy knight. In the Welsh romance, Peredur too is given a sword by the owner of the first castle that he visits. He uses the sword to strike an iron column and is told that he has not yet come into his full strength. Gawain sees a broken sword on the bier next to a dead knight and tries to repair it. Sometimes the sword is identified as the one used to behead John the Baptist, a not unexpected development once the cup and the spear became associated with the biblical relics. Galahad also receives a sword. Sometimes it was placed on Solomon's ship and is destined for him, and sometimes he draws it from a floating stone.

The spear in the grail procession is usually identified with the legend of Longinus, the Roman centurion converted to Christianity after he pierced Christ's side at the time of the Crucifixion. However, it can have a more varied function in grail processions. In some grail romances the blood flowing from the spear is so profuse that it is channelled into pipes. In *Perlesvaus* two maidens carry the grail and the lance, which bleeds into the cup in which Joseph had collected

Christ's blood. In *Peredur* it is a huge spear which has wounded his cousin and from which flow streams of blood.

The final lady in Chrétien's grail procession carries an elaborate plate (*tailleor*) made of silver. In later romances this is identified as a paten, a flat metal dish that covered the chalice during mass. The meaning of the dish is most fully explained in the *Continuations* of Gerbert and Manessier. Joseph covers the grail after he has collected Christ's blood clearly foreshadowing the sacrament of the Eucharist. In some versions, Perceval's mother is among believers who accompanied the grail to Britain, and she is said to have carried the plate, but this object never becomes as important as the grail, lance or sword.

The earliest medieval grail romance presented readers with a shining jewelled object, but did not clarify the nature of the grail. Chrétien hinted that the Fisher King was sustained by sacred food, and the mysterious nature of this food may have prompted Robert de Boron to introduce the idea that the grail was the cup used at the Last Supper. Most subsequent romances follow this identification. Thus the grail became associated with sustenance, with a wounded king and with the Christian sacrament of the Eucharist. By extension, the bleeding lance in this mysterious procession became identified with the Lance of Longinus, which drew the last of Christ's blood as he hung on the cross. Malory's account of the Dolorous Blow and the conception of Galahad provide background to the grail story, and he emphasized the link between the grail and medieval ideas about the Holy Blood. Malory incorporates material from many earlier grail romances and attempts to resolve the complexity of these themes, but even he left a few details unexplained.

The grail story changed over time, it became both more complex and more Christianised, but it never resolved itself into a single narrative. This is no doubt due in great part to the differences in aims and intentions of the romance writers themselves. What emerged is a dense and fascinating story which was to provide the basis for new visions of the grail in the centuries that followed.

VISIONS OF THE GRAIL

I N THE TALE OF *Peredur fab Efrog*,[1] two young men enter a hall carrying a huge spear with streams of blood flowing from it while two maidens carry a large salver containing a bloody head. This procession, witnessed by the young hero Peredur son of Efrog, has been identified with the grail. It is one of the medieval tales from *The Mabinogion*, and as a Welsh language text, it is the only description of the grail written originally in a Celtic language. However, the object containing the bloody head is described as a *disgyl* and the term 'grail' does not appear.

Lady Charlotte Guest's influential translation of *The Mabinogion* in the nineteenth century encouraged new interest in Arthurian tradition and in Welsh literature. Guest's romantic attitude to chivalry as a code that inspired noble behaviour reflected Victorian pride in its British heritage.[2] By this time, the Celts, and this included the Welsh, were an important component in the emergence of this new British identity. Before Guest's translation of the *Peredur* romance made this Welsh version of the grail legend available to a wider public, the poet Robert Southey published an introduction to a new critical edition of Malory's *Le Morte Darthur* (1817).[3] Both editors looked to the chivalric romances of the Middle Ages for evidence of a nobility of character at variance with their own age. The interplay between chivalric romance and high ideals, specifically the qualities of Christian piety, is an important theme in the poetry of Alfred Lord Tennyson, undoubtedly the most famous reworking of the Arthurian legend in Victorian literature. Ten years after the first publication of *The Idylls of the King*, Tennyson added his treatment of the Holy Grail theme.[4] His poetry inspired many other writers and artists. For Tennyson the grail quest was linked to the unravelling of the Arthurian world. The American poet James Russell Lowell also extended the meaning of the grail beyond the world of medieval Christianity.[5] This marked a shift of interest to the inner world of the knights and to a new perspective on the meaning of faith, rather than the spiritual reality of the grail.

There was also considerable interest in the origin and meaning of the grail legend that focused on the Celts as an important source of inspiration. That the grail originated in the mythological traditions of the Celts has been one of the most influential theories about its origin. The Welsh tale of *Peredur* seemed to provide a transitional stage between an original Celtic myth and the Breton poets who inspired the French grail romances. The *Peredur* tale apparently combined motifs scattered throughout other Mabinogion tales. For example a life-giving cauldron of regeneration (*pair dadeni*) is mentioned in *Branwen*. Her brother, Bendigeidfran, is mortally wounded with a spear, but his decapitated head magically presides at two Otherworld feasts. In the tale of *Manawydan*, his kingdom is laid waste by a magic curse, and Manawydan's wife and stepson are trapped in the Otherworld after touching a magic bowl. In *Owein or the Lady of the Well*, the hero defeats an armed warrior who appears when water is poured from a bowl chained to a magic well. Magic vessels are among the treasures sought in *Culhwch and Olwen*, and the tale of *Lludd and Llefelys* describes a scream heard every May Day that is so horrific, it causes barrenness.[6] Although these motifs fulfil different roles in the medieval tales, theories about Celtic origin viewed them as late survivals of an ancient myth about a goddess of sovereignty who bestowed a magic cauldron on a hero. The successful union of the hero and the goddess produced abundance and fertility, while failure resulted in barrenness. Cauldrons have been explained as the pagan precursors of the grail itself and barrenness as an early image of the wasteland theme in the grail romances. The bloody head was related to a pagan Celtic cult of the head, and Bendigeidfran was seen as an early version of Bran the wounded Fisher King. As a result the procession in the *Peredur* romance was regarded as an ancient form of the grail myth and, for some, Wales played a pivotal role in the creation of the Grail myth.[7]

There is however, no extant account of such a myth. As a result, incidents in later texts like *The Mabinogion* have been used to reconstruct what an early myth might have been like. Alfred Nutt's seminal work, *The Holy Grail with Especial Reference to its Celtic Origin*,[8] identified the grail story with a Celtic myth about a sacred otherworldly object. The author examined stories about magic Otherworld vessels and compared them with folktales about heroes who searched for supernatural objects or underwent adventures in order to marry supernatural women. He believed that the 'oral' traditions of the Celts from Ireland, Scotland, Wales, Cornwall and Brittany preserved elements of this myth and were the ultimate source for the grail story. Nutt's ideas were consistent with the belief that pagan Celtic tradition survived into the Christian era, and his view of oral transmission provided a neat mechanism for the transformation of pagan myth into Christian romance. It also explained away any inconsistencies between early Celtic tales and the medieval grail story as a failure by medieval authors to understand the underlying myth. Speculations about the pagan ritual origins of the grail reached a wider audience through the influential work of the American scholar Jessie Weston. For her, an esoteric initiation ceremony, related to ancient mystery religions and theosophical beliefs, lay behind references to the cycle of seasons, fertility and replacement of rulers in grail romances.[9] A new vision of the grail was emerging, one which shifted the emphasis from the knights and their adventures to the nature of the grail itself.

The figure of the Fisher King is important in Celtic and ritual visions of the grail. In Chrétien's romance, he is called Le Roi Pecheur, but he has been interpreted subsequently as a Celtic deity or an ancient ritual figure. Robert de Boron's romances give further details about this figure. Before the grail was taken to Britain, Hebron (Bron), the brother-in-law of Joseph of Arimathea, caught a fish and placed it on the grail table. Bron is called the Rich Fisher or the Fisher King after he becomes lord of the Grail Castle in Britain, and his son, Alain also becomes a Fisher King. In some romances this figure is identified with the Grail King. The Fisher/Grail King is often wounded or sick and can only be healed when the preordained visitor to his castle asks the proper question. Sometimes the king's sickness is reflected in the state of his kingdom, which has become a wasteland. In the earliest grail romance, Perceval's failure to ask the question means that the king's wound is not healed, and the land remains undefended, but the text does not suggest that the land has become waste because the king is wounded. Although the link between the king and land differs depending on the romance, in ritual interpretations, it is always interpreted as a sign of the mythic dependence between the king and the land. In contemporary literature the wasteland motif has been used as a metaphor for the alienation and the emptiness of modern materialism.[10] In his notes to *The Waste Land*, T. S. Eliot acknowledged Jessie Weston's influence in his choice of title and use of symbolism within the poem.[11] The Phoenician Sailor in Madame Sosostris's Tarot card reading and the man fishing in the dirty canal thinking of kings (lines 185–92) suggest Perceval's host, the Fisher King, and there are other allusions to the grail romances such as the empty chapel (lines 296–393) and the dry wasted land with its departed nymphs (line 175). The Tarot card reading also reflects the work of the occult scholar and Arthurian critic, A. E. Waite, who wrote several books on the grail placing it in a tradition of mysticism which extended beyond even the Celts.[12] Eliot later repudiated such references, but critical reception of the poem was sympathetic to the idea of fertility rite when it first appeared,[13] while many of his contemporaries as well as more recent authors have drawn on similar ideas.

A contemporary of Eliot and student of the occult, Mary Butts, incorporated ideas about seasonal rituals of renewal centred on the grail in her novel, *Armed with Madness*.[14] In the third novel of C. S. Lewis's science fiction trilogy, *That Hideous Strength*, the hero, Ransom, who goes by the name Mr Fisher King and has an injured foot, returns to the earthly but still mythic world of modern Oxford University. The novel is not about the grail as such, but the Wasteland and the Fisher King had a particular meaning for Lewis as metaphors for humanity's struggle against the sterile materialism of the modern world.[15] Several of Naomi Mitchison's novels incorporated ideas about ritual seasonal renewal, and in *To the Chapel Perilous*,[16] this ritualized world is given an Arthurian context. A. A. Attanasio's *The Serpent and the Grail*, part of his *Arthor* series, also recasts the Arthurian grail quest in terms of a wounded king connected to his land.[17] In Dorothy Roberts's *Kinsmen of the Grail*, an older Gawain takes on the role comparable to the old Grail King in Weston's ritual myth who eventually gives way to the younger Perceval.[18]

The grail was a significant image for the Anglo-Welsh poet and artist David Jones. Although not a Welsh speaker, he retained a strong sense of his Welsh heritage and identified closely with the Arthurian legend both as the native myth of Wales, and as the common intellectual heritage of all Britons. Many images in his striking and original work are drawn from Welsh Arthurian sources, while the Eucharist also provided a rich seam of images for this Roman Catholic convert. Jones served with the Royal Welch Fusiliers during the First World War, and his war experiences, like so many British poets of his generation, deeply affected his art and poetry. All these influences found voice in poems such as *In Parenthesis* (1937), *The Anathemata* (1952) and *The Sleeping Lord* (1974).[19] The elegiac tone of the poetry, the sense of alienation from a cultural wellspring and the search for a way to reverse this loss through myth echo Eliot's evocation of the grail in *The Waste Land*. In his war poem *In Parenthesis*, Jones describes the Western Front as a 'burial yard' without light; terms which reflect both the wasteland and the journey to the Chapel Perilous. Empty and threatening though it is, this wasteland, like that in the grail myth, can be transformed by rediscovering, and more importantly, by re-enacting the myth of Arthur and the Grail. In *The Sleeping Lord* Jones evokes the candles and the spear in the grail procession in order to identify Arthur, the sleeping hero, with the maimed king of the grail myth. The ultimate question posed by the poem is whether the land is waiting for the sleeping lord or is 'the wasted land' itself the sleeping lord? The winter setting, the time when the 'dying god' of the ritual was inactive and awaiting resurrection, reinforces this.[20]

In the first section of *The Anathemata*, 'Rite and Fore-time', ancient ritual reinforces Christian theology in a seamless cultural continuity. 'The cult-man' who stands alone in 'Pellam's land', the wasteland of Malory's *Le Morte Darthur*, is a timeless archetype lost in a modern wasteland, but the poem also identifies the grail castle with the institution of the Eucharist, 'the holy dysshe'[21] Jones, like Eliot, turns to the ritual grail theories of writers like Jessie Weston to provide a means of understanding the meaning of the grail in the twentieth century.[22] The grail quest was the supreme achievement of the Arthurian world, but it was for Jones a quintessentially Christian quest, expressed in the context of an ancient initiation ritual with the power to reunite the maimed king with the land through the actions of a hero. In the complex multi-layered world of his poetry, the grail hero who heals the king merges with the Maimed King and with Christ as Redeemer of creation.[23]

The revival of interest in the grail, and in Arthurian tradition generally, has had a continuing impact on British art and literature since the nineteenth century, but there are comparatively few Welsh-language treatments of the subject, although John Dyfnallt Owen's poem on the Holy Grail won the Crown at the National Eisteddfod in 1907.[24] The Wesleyan Methodist minister and writer, Edward Tegla Davies wrote a booklet for young readers called Y *Greal Sanctaidd* that traced the history of the grail from medieval text to modern literature with an emphasis on its spiritual meaning and relevance to Welsh life.[25] The distinctiveness of Tegla's book lies in the fact that it was aimed at a young audience, but the link between the grail and Welsh Christianity runs through almost all interpretations of the grail in Wales. For writers like Dyfnallt and Tegla, conversion to Christianity dramatically changed the world-view of early Wales. For the Anglo-Welsh writer Arthur Machen, on the other hand, the grail was the central talisman of Celtic Christianity in Wales.

Arthur Machen was born the son of the Anglican vicar of the village of Llandewi Fach, near Caerleon in south Wales, in 1863. He was profoundly affected by the landscape of his childhood: the Gwent countryside, the Black Mountains, the ancient Wentwood Forest, and Caerleon itself. Haunted landscape and ancient history merged in his writing to produce both the dark forces of his horror fiction and the mystical esotericism of his writing about the grail. The materialism of modern society profoundly disturbed Machen, and this comes through clearly in The Secret Glory. The alienated central character, the schoolboy Ambrose Meyrick, finds salvation from the spiritually barren and materialistic world through Celtic Christianity and 'the most glorious Quest and Adventure of the Sangraal'.[26] He also 'speaks of a Celtic cup which had been preserved in one family for many hundreds of years'. On the death of the last keeper this cup was placed in Meyrick's hands. This Welsh relic, kept by a Welsh guardian, echoes legends about early Welsh saints as well as later traditions about the Nanteos cup.[27] Machen's interpretation of the grail favoured a close connection to the native Christianity of Wales and his clever references to traditions about the Nanteos cup give it a specifically Welsh context.[28]

The mystic experience of the grail imbues the atmosphere of another Machen short story, 'The Great Return', in which a sceptical journalist investigates the sudden recovery of a dying girl who had a vision of three men holding a bell, a glowing altar, and a cup respectively. The Welsh saints David, Teilo and Beuno, and their sacred relics, a bell, a cup and an altar, are commemorated in a fictional church dedicated to three saints, Llantrisant, located on the Welsh coast.[29] Machen believed that the grail was originally a holy relic of the Celtic Church and embodied the real and ecstatic Celtic Christianity in Wales prior to the advent of the Latin Church.[30] It is worth noting, in this context, the Welsh aspect of Machen's fictionalized account of a personal experience in London which was, although he does not say so specifically, a vision of the Holy Grail. After the death of his first wife, a devastated Machen teetered on the edge of breakdown. In a sketch of despair and depression called *The Holy Things* (1897), the everyday experiences of bells, lamplight and traffic in the city are transformed into the smell of incense and a choir of angels singing in Welsh by a man walking down Holborn in London.[31] Machen's wanderings through London and his psychological recovery were couched in the same terms of spiritual and sensory experience which he used to such good effect in his writing and which recall the experiences of the grail knights in the medieval romances. He saw parallels between the lives of St David and Joseph of Arimathea, and believed that grail romances were based on the wanderings of Welsh saints. For Machen the meaning of the 'Sangraal … the holy thing that healed all hurts and doles'[32] was the essence of Celtic Christianity. It was a view shared by many of his contemporaries. Interest at that time focused on whether the episodes of the grail quest constituted a single narrative, and if so, what was its original meaning and purpose. A consensus favoured a myth about a Celtic talisman associated with abundance, and the newly edited texts of Irish and Welsh tales and the existence of a rich Celtic folk heritage, whose narrative themes resembled those in medieval literary texts, came to be regarded as the sources of the grail romances.

Another important theme in Celtic and ritual interpretations of the grail is the connection between male characters and a mysterious female figure sometimes identified as a sovereignty goddess, the supernatural consort of the rightful ruler. The physical appearance of the sovereignty goddess mirrors the health of the kingdom and the fitness of the king, and she is ugly and beautiful by turns. Sovereignty is allegedly represented in the grail romances by the loathly lady who berates the grail hero for his failure and by various beautiful women who help him and assume the role of consort. None of the romances indicates that the loathly lady becomes beautiful as the result of the grail knight's actions. However, the double nature of the sovereignty goddess is one of the 'missing' elements necessary to create a hypothetical link between medieval romance and the Celtic myths that supposedly preceded them, and the idea remains popular.[33] In *The White Goddess* Robert Graves equated the grail with the cauldron of this pagan Celtic sovereignty goddess.[34] Several modern fantasy novels incorporate elements of this to create a more feminist perception of the grail. Both Marion Zimmer Bradley's *The Mists of Avalon*[35] and Rosalind Miles's *The Child of the Holy Grail*[36] depict the early Arthurian world as a struggle between pagan goddess mystery religion and the incursions of repressive Christianity. The film *Excalibur* exploits this theme and Perceval achieves his quest when he realizes that King Arthur and the land are one. He returns to Camelot and revives the king with liquid from the grail whereupon the land bursts into flower.[37]

In some modern treatments of the legend, the female characters have merged with notions of the sacred feminine and speculations about a lost goddess culture repressed by Christianity. The figure of Mary Magdalene as the hidden bride of Christ has come to represent this lost sacred feminine in many modern conspiracy treatments of the grail.[38] This blend of poetic imagination and scholarship is familiar today in works of alternative history, but the idea of a conspiracy aimed at suppressing an alternative Christianity has entered grail fiction. Secrets guarded by mystic groups like the Templars and the

Freemasons were added to ideas about ancient fertility myths, and alternative theories were a major influence in this changing emphasis. In Bernard Cornwell's *The Warlord Chronicles* written in the 1990s, the grail originates in the sacred cauldron of Celtic folklore and echoes the idea of a Celtic pagan religion in an Arthurian setting. His later trilogy, *The Grail Quest* has a very different grail.[39] It begins with the theft of a sacred lance and its central character is an unknown descendant of a noble family who were lords in the Languedoc during the crusade against the Cathars. In Kate Mosse's novel, *Labyrinth*,[40] a young woman archaeologist finds mysterious symbols inscribed on the walls of a cave in southern France. This time-shift thriller eventually reveals her connection to a young woman who guarded the secret of the Holy Grail during the Cathar Crusade.

Throughout its history and throughout the many changing interpretations of the grail from Tennyson onwards, the themes of the grail romances retain their power to engage our imagination. As a symbol of personal transformation and cultural renewal, the grail continues to fascinate us, and today the Internet plays a role in the appeal of these legends. Besides the growing number of websites that offer comment on the grail, code-breaking and quest plots provide formats for computer, video and role-play games. The well-established *Pendragon* fantasy role-play game uses the grail as a storyline in a context which exploits multiple references to Arthurian and Celtic themes.[41] In the Games Workshop scenario, *Queen Victoria and the Holy Grail*, a mysterious theft from Buckingham Palace reveals the British Monarchy as 'the guardians of a gold chalice reputedly the true Holy Grail.'[42] The context for the Gabriel Knight games series revolves around a book dealer with supernatural powers. *Gabriel Knight 3: Blood of the Sacred, Blood of the Damned*[43] is set in the alternative grail country of southern France. Video and role-play gaming now regularly combine themes from grail conspiracy thrillers and traditional quest plot structures with science fiction, anime animation and other aspects of popular culture.

Themes in grail romance resonate with Celtic tales about food producing vessels, however it is difficult to reduce the romances to a single source and attempts to reconstruct a coherent earlier narrative are invariably speculative. Theories about the Celtic origin of the grail depend on hypothetical reconstructions of what the original myth might have been rather than on direct textual evidence. The thread that connects scholarship, alternative writing and fiction is the belief that the romances contained mythic elements that could be recovered and could illuminate a genuine mythic source. More recently attention has focused on existing texts rather than reconstructions and this has shifted the emphasis to the historical context in which the romances were written. However, the Celts were, and still remain, a fashionable embodiment of romantic 'otherness'. David Jones's poetic and artistic interpretations of the grail legend were published in the middle of the twentieth century. His work draws on his experiences in the First World War modulated by his personal response to Welsh tradition. Only a decade before that war, the first published account identifying the Nanteos cup with the Grail appeared. It combined a romantic view of the past with extreme sentimentality, and it localized the legend in a Welsh context. Scholarship at that time focused on wider Celtic connections and pagan origins.

Earlier grail scholarship tended to view the romances as the survivals of a far older tradition often linked to Celtic myths about a pagan grail and a pre-Christian fertility ritual that it was supposed to contain. The belief that the pagan world survived secretly into the Christian Middle Ages is an attractive metaphor that provided both a meaning for the grail and a means to expose the failures of contemporary society. The pattern of code, revelation and secret message that repeats itself endlessly in modern grail traditions offers us a connection to the ancient past. There is, however, little to support the idea that such secrets and mysteries ever actually existed, and the numerous historians who take issue with the assumptions behind these theories have a point. The attraction of this alternative view is that it places the grail at the centre of a web of religious vision, millennial anxiety and nostalgic reimagining supported by a mix of science, pseudo-science, and popular culture. As a result, the past can be reclaimed and the present overcome in order to usher in a new era of harmony and spiritual fulfilment. Grail narratives have become charged with new layers of meaning, and modern grail legends now reach a global audience through digital mass media, print and television.

The alternative books of the 1980s, modern conspiracy thrillers, fantasy novels and computer games have undoubtedly created new audiences. Speculations about pagan fertility rituals and ancient myths provided rich poetic metaphors for new grail literature, while alternative theories about the meaning of the grail worked their way into the important market for popular books. This new vision of the Holy Grail can accommodate concepts of pluralism and tolerance, secret wisdom and individual enlightenment. At the same time, it coincided with interest in non-Christian spirituality and the engagement of self so characteristic of modern forms of neo-paganism. It presented an attractive and imaginative vision of an alternate world onto which it is possible to project a multitude of meanings, and it illustrates the process by which a cultural theory can be transformed into belief.[44] The grail as a way to expose negative aspects of the modern world, to express positive ideas about a balanced society, or as a defence against conspiracy now crosses the boundaries of literary, artistic, popular and even academic imagination. This fascination with the grail in which academic and quasi-academic approaches intertwined is important for understanding the many facets of the legend in today's world.

FROM WALES TO GLASTONBURY

THE REGION SURROUNDING Glastonbury Tor in Somerset has become a focal point for modern grail legends associated with alternative spirituality. The Abbey at Glastonbury was among the richest religious houses in England until a disastrous fire in 1184. Pilgrimages to venerate the relics of important saints had provided the Abbey with income and prestige. After the fire, new cults associated with King Arthur, Joseph of Arimathea and the grail helped re-establish the Abbey's position. The process began with the finding of Arthur's grave in 1191 and continued with the development of the Joseph of Arimathea legend in the fifteenth century. Both cults provided links between medieval Arthurian traditions and the Abbey's earlier importance. Long-standing rivalries with other religious centres eventually weakened Glastonbury, but its fortunes revived in the twentieth century when the Church of England purchased the Abbey ruins, and the Chalice Well area at the foot of Glastonbury Tor developed into a modern alternative spiritual centre. This period coincided with the emergence of a group of individuals who identified themselves, through the legendary history of St Joseph, with a number of mystical ideas about the grail. Modern traditions about Glastonbury and the grail had begun.

The association of Glastonbury as the resting place of Joseph of Arimathea is a relatively late feature of the grail romances. The Abbey, however, was an established Benedictine monastery by the seventh century. After a series of Viking raids, it was repaired and enlarged during the tenth century and became a centre for Saxon religious life. After the Normans arrived in the eleventh century, the new abbots were keen to maintain and extend its prestige. At the beginning of the twelfth century, Abbot Henry of Blois commissioned the historian and monk William of Malmesbury to write *De Antiquitate Glastoniensis Ecclesiae*. This is the earliest history of the Abbey based on material in its well-stocked library, William's own observations and, no doubt, information from the monks themselves. Some of the material is undoubtedly legend intended to enhance Glastonbury's position, but William was a careful historian, and much of his account has been confirmed by archaeology.[1] William accepted that the Abbey was founded before St Augustine's mission to convert the English in 597, but there is nothing of Arthur, Joseph of Arimathea or the grail, which suggests that these were not part of Glastonbury's real or legendary history when William wrote his account.

Legends helped Glastonbury maintain its status, and the traditions concerning Arthur, Joseph and the grail reflect its continuing attempts to attract patronage and maintain its influence. While the fire undoubtedly provided a catalyst for new legends, both Geoffrey of Monmouth and Gerald of Wales hint at Glastonbury's connection with the Celtic Otherworld. Geoffrey of Monmouth refers to *insula Auallonis* (the Isle of Avalon) or *insula pomorum* (the Isle of Apples), although he does not link it specifically with Glastonbury. However, Gerald of Wales does identify *insula avallonis* with the region around Glastonbury Tor. The name Glastonbury was derived from the glassy blue colour of the river, and *glas* in English was equated with *gwydyr* in Welsh, hence *Ynys Wydrin* (the Island of Glass). The identification of Avalon with Glastonbury is central to ideas about its sacredness as it reinforces the assumption that traditions, no matter how recent, are grounded in the world of British myth, specifically the areas now occupied by Wales, Cornwall and Brittany. The Welsh name was probably invented to explain the English one illustrating how problematic is the assumption that early Celtic sources lie behind later Arthurian traditions. However, the identification of Glastonbury with Avalon, the burial place of the king, established the story of Arthur as a national myth by localizing it in British geography.

The mix of ecclesiastical and secular legends also affected the development of the Holy Grail tradition. William's original account was expanded several times as Glastonbury's wealth and importance grew. By the mid-thirteenth century, the expanded version contained much of the legendary history of Glastonbury that we know today. It began with the supposed arrival of twelve missionary hermits under St Joseph of Arimathea in the first century of the Christian era. A sympathetic pagan king, Arviragus, granted the missionaries land around Glastonbury Tor, where they built the first Christian church in Britain. After the death of the last hermit, the site reverted to wilderness until another pagan, King Lucius, helped rebuild the original church. At the beginning of the fifth century, Patrick, later confused with the apostle to Ireland, became the first abbot of a proper monastery, Glastonbury Abbey. A charter attributed to this Patrick provided a popular alternative to William of Malmesbury's sober history. It incorporated the role of Joseph of Arimathea as founder of Glastonbury and custodian of the grail into an ostensibly historical charter, despite the fact that the Joseph material came from secular grail romances. In support of this, a later version of the *De Antiquitate* cited a foundation charter listing a number of saints whose relics were at Glastonbury, among them Bridget, Gildas, David and Columba. The source for this convenient information was a mysterious book supposedly found by Abbot Patrick in the ancient church dedicated to St Michael on Glastonbury Tor. There is no mention of this foundation charter in William of Malmesbury's original account. By the thirteenth-century, however, traditions about King Arthur were associated with the Abbey, and the apocryphal legends about Joseph had become part of the grail romances. With the aid of this suspiciously convenient charter, Joseph of Arimathea was added to the Abbey's foundation legends and transformed into an early missionary who carried the Christian message to the West.[2]

Joseph of Arimathea is mentioned in the four New Testament gospel accounts as a holy man who obtained Christ's body from Pontius Pilate and buried it in his own tomb. Apocryphal gospels such as the *Gospel of Nicodemus* added details about how Joseph's faith miraculously sustained him in prison, and how he and his companions carried the Christian message westwards into Europe. Joseph entered the grail romances in Robert de Boron's work which specified, for the first time, that the grail was the vessel used at the Last Supper and that Joseph, after a number of adventures, travelled westwards to a place called 'vaus D'Avaron'. Robert de Boron wrote at the end of the twelfth century, about the time Arthur's grave became part of the Glastonbury pilgrim experience and 'vaus D'Avaron' became equated with Avalon, and by extension Glastonbury. Joseph's brief appearances in the Gospels were expanded in the Apocrypha accounts. Other grail romances, the *Continuations* of Chrètien's *Perceval*, the *Perlesvaus*, the *Vulgate Cycle* or the *Lancelot Grail* developed Joseph's British connections and furthered his links with the grail and its guardians. In the French Grail romances, he became associated with the cup of the Last Supper, while sources such as the later additions to William of Malmesbury's history, stress his role as an early missionary bringing Christianity to Britain. Robert de Boron calls Joseph *decurio*, in effect a knight, and therefore an appropriate role model for the five grail knights, Perceval, Gawain, Lancelot, Bors and Galahad.

The popularity of the Joseph legend at Glastonbury coincided with a period when the Abbey's power and influence, under Abbot John Chinnock (1375–1420) was at its height. Chinnock commissioned a local monk, John of Glastonbury, to write *Chronica sive antiquitates Glastonienses Ecclesie* (The Antiquities of the Abbey), which depicted Joseph and his followers as the founders of Glastonbury. John of Glastonbury even cited a fictional Welsh prophet named Melkin on the location of Joseph of Arimathea's tomb. He is also the first to mention two white and silver vessels (*duo fassula alba et argentea cruore*) containing the blood and sweat of Jesus. The legend linked the saint with the national hero, King Arthur, and the historical arguments centred on Joseph's conversion of Britain rather than his connection with the grail. So influential was this new legend that the English king ordered a search for Joseph's body, although nothing was actually found.[3]

In the fourteenth century an English chronicle writer, John Hardyng combined the Glastonbury tradition and the story of the grail knight, Galahad. Like so many proponents of dubious grail theories, Hardyng invoked the supposed antiquity of the story of Joseph of Arimathea to substantiate his claims. In his version, Joseph converted a pagan king, Arviragus, who gave him the land

54

on which Glastonbury Abbey was founded. Later Joseph presented Arviragus with a shield inscribed with a red cross. In Arthurian literature, Galahad's arms have a red cross, but Hardyng adds details of his own, namely that Galahad found the shield in Avalon (i.e. Glastonbury) and carried it during his grail quest to the Holy Land where he founded a chivalric order, the Sanke Roiall (i.e. the Holy Blood). Hardyng was a soldier rather than a scholar with little interest in the grail as a Eucharistic symbol. He demystified the grail and interpreted it as 'royal blood' (Sanke Roiall). By translating *sangreal* as 'royal blood' and associating Galahad with a chivalric order, Hardyng anticipated one of the most popular modern ideas about the grail, namely that it was not an object at all, but a person whose descendants make up 'a holy bloodline'. One final detail was needed to complete the Joseph legend and another English writer, Henry Lovelich supplied this by adding that Joseph was buried in 'the abbey of Glas ... / which Abbey of Glastyngbery now men hald'.[4]

The legendary story of St Joseph at Glastonbury proved extremely useful. It helped maintain the political importance of Glastonbury during the Middle Ages. From the sixteenth century onwards, it provided the English Reformation with ancient roots for British Christianity, and it is equally appropriate as a foundation legend for the ecologically sound, pro-pagan institutions of the modern Celtic revival. The revival of interest in the Arthurian legend in the late nineteenth century, coupled with an interest in Christian spiritual renewal, gave birth to a new esoteric and mystical view of Glastonbury as the successor to the pagan Avalon. This new layer to the myth expanded Joseph of Arimathea's early Christian foundation at Glastonbury, a place once known as 'the Isle of Avalon' and Arthur's burial site, to include an ancient goddess place, a centre for the sacred feminine. The Bath and Wells Diocesan Trust took charge of Glastonbury Abbey in 1909, and this ushered in a new era for a mystic vision of Glastonbury. The grail was an essential part of this vision. For some it was a Christian relic, for others a pagan talisman or an occult force, but all believed in the power of the grail to transform the present and future.

The link between Glastonbury and Avalon has become so well established that many visitors feel there is little doubt that it was a pagan centre before it was Christian. These are potent forces in contemporary Glastonbury, but they are highly speculative. Neither the archaeological excavations nor references in Arthurian literature support the idea that Glastonbury was a druid stronghold or a primitive Celtic church with a nature-oriented cosmology. The creative thread which links these assumptions is the story of the Holy Grail in which the apocryphal legend of Joseph of Arimathea was fused with the medieval grail romances into an apparently historical narrative about ancient Glastonbury. This has provided fertile ground for the development of modern grail legends in which Glastonbury is part of the western Celtic world that includes Wales, Cornwall and parts of Somerset. These new grail traditions provide an identity available for all, no matter to which nation they belong, and they have created new links between Glastonbury and Wales.

Just before the turn of the twentieth century, a psychic vision prompted Dr John Goodchild to conceal an antique glass bowl, which he had acquired in Italy, in some waste ground on the outskirts of Glastonbury where it was eventually retrieved by the Tudor Pole family and their friends. Goodchild's book *The Light of the West: An Account of the Dannite Settlement of Ireland*[5] suggested that the Tuatha De Danann of Irish mythology were in fact historical inhabitants of ancient Ireland who, in the person of their High Queen, Mor Rigan or St Bride, venerated the female aspect of the Deity. The teachings of the druids were derived from this pre-Christian mystery cult. Knowledge of the Mor Rigan as a real queen had been lost leaving only the memory of a battlefield goddess, but the veneration of the sacred feminine had been passed on to the figure of Bride (St Bridget). The mystical overtones to his antiquarian interests forged heretofore unknown esoteric connections between spiritual and secular realms at the dawn of western civilization. In Goodchild's spiritual world, the pagan female divinity symbolized by the cauldron (i.e. grail) blended with the male principle of Christianity, the sword of Christ. The idea that goddess worship was central to Celtic paganism and that the Celtic Church was sympathetic to this feminist paganism has become influential in modern spirituality movements, especially at Glastonbury.

Goodchild believed in a matriarchal, druidical Christianity with centres in Ireland, Rome, and most crucially for the development of the modern history of the Holy Grail, at Glastonbury itself. He never called the glass curio purchased in Italy the Holy Grail, but he believed that would play a crucial role in redressing the imbalance between masculine and feminine spirituality. His theories about coded pictorial images, hidden messages in architecture and literature and mysterious links between mythical and historical figures anticipate by nearly a century some of the ideas which have found their way into modern grail theories and novels, most notably perhaps *The Da Vinci Code* and *Labyrinth*.[6] Lack of evidence for this goddess-centred civilization, then as now, was overcome by asserting that everything had to be disguised in the face of hostile Christianity (i.e. Latin Christianity). Deliberate concealment in the face of a hostile force is another common feature of the legend pattern which appears repeatedly in modern grail legends.

Just before *The Light of the West* was published in 1898, Goodchild had a vision about 'The Cup' (as he referred to it) he had concealed at Bride's Well outside Glastonbury. Several years later, he visited the site with his friend and fellow Celtic enthusiast, Fiona MacLeod, a pseudonym for the Scottish writer William Sharp. Sharp dedicated a book to Dr Goodchild who shared his enthusiasm for a Celtic spirituality based on reverence for a female divinity who presided over the world of nature.[7] A young Bristol woman, Katherine Tudor Pole, her brother, Wellesley Tudor Pole (1884–1968) and their friends, Janet and Christine Allen 'discovered' the Cup in September 1906. Initially at least, Tudor Pole and his friends believed that it was the Holy Grail of legend. Wellesley Tudor Pole's millennial leanings invoked the wisdom of the grail, initiates of ancient mystery religions, and the expectation of a New Age and echoed the ideas of Goodchild and Sharp. Experts who examined the curious object were cautious, but not dismissive, about an early date for the glass bowl. They included Archdeacon Basil Wilberforce, grandson of the anti-slavery campaigner, the American novelist Mark Twain and Sir William Crookes, scientist, specialist in glass and a president of the Society for Psychical Research. However, as is so often the case with attempts to date relics, expert opinion never reached a consensus, nor did it resolve the contradictions between the history of the glass curio from St Bride's Well and the St Joseph legend. Opinion favoured a modern date for the object from St Bride's Well, but just enough ambiguity remained, so those who were inclined to believe could feel there was a possibility that the object might be the authentic grail.[8]

After Goodchild's death in 1914, this circle of friends went on to other things. Wellesley Tudor Pole served in both World Wars and founded the Chalice Well Trust at Glastonbury in 1959. Christine Allen, who had married the Scottish painter John Duncan, returned to be the first Warden. The bowl was given to the Chalice Well Trust after Tudor Pole's death in 1968, where it remains. The establishment of this Trust involved another pioneer in the Glastonbury revival, Alice Buckton (1867–1944). The Chal(c)welle at Glastonbury had become Chalice Well, the final resting place of the grail, even though the site was associated with the eighteenth-century vogue for 'drinking the waters' rather than medieval pilgrimage activity. The establishment of a convent school there in the 1880s contributed to this sense of long-standing religious history. Buckton established a centre for theatre and the arts at Chalice Well in the belief that artistic and aesthetic sensibility opened a channel to spiritual enlightenment. It was her wish that the site become an international centre for healing and spirituality, but these plans were never fully realized until the Chalice Well Trust acquired it in 1959. Frederick Bligh Bond's cover for the actual well site embodies the symbolic meaning that Glastonbury has acquired in contemporary culture. The curving art nouveau plant designs combined with the interlocking yin-yang symbols of male and female spirituality fuse eastern thinking and Celtic magic into an eclectic spirituality.[9] The spring at Chalice Well became a popular destination for visitors. In addition, St Bride's Well on the outskirts of the town, where Goodchild concealed his cup, has become associated with modern goddess worship. Another popular event at Glastonbury today is the Goddess Conference held annually in July. Costumed processions around Glastonbury Tor and Chalice Well, plus numerous workshops celebrate the traditions of sacred feminism that began with the revival of Glastonbury at the beginning of the twentieth century.[10]

Many of Alice Buckton's attitudes to the spiritual potential of art overlapped with those of Frederick Bligh Bond (1864–1945), an architect whose work followed the principles of the Arts and Craft movement and who was associated with early archaeological excavations at Glastonbury Abbey.[11] Bond took up a post to oversee the excavations at the Abbey in 1908, under the auspices of the local archaeological society. He was also a member of the Society for Psychical Research, and inevitably his attempts to recover information about the Abbey through psychic channelling created tension. It was his belief that builders at Glastonbury had used occult *gematria*, an ancient science of sacred geometry based on hidden mathematical formulas found in the Bible. While Bond and Goodchild discussed these ideas, there were differences in their approach. Dr Goodchild and his circle blended Christianity with elements of Celtic paganism, but Bligh Bond's assertions always remained within the context of Christianity. His psychic researches rigorously followed the principles of the Society for Psychical Research, and he truly believed that messages from long dead monks helped him locate features on the Abbey site. Like many who sympathised with the principles of the Arts and Crafts movement, he viewed the medieval period from a rather romantic and mystical perspective. However, his belief that Glastonbury was a 'cipher in stone' built according to sacred geometry, caused him to fall out with both Church authorities and archaeologists and he was replaced. Initially Bond had been sceptical about the cup found at St Bride's and did not immediately connect the Abbey with the grail. However in subsequent accounts of archaeological ciphers and automatic writings such as *The Glastonbury Scripts* published in the 1920s, he accepted the connection between the Abbey and the quest for the grail.[12]

Another contributor to mythic Glastonbury was born Violet Mary Firth in Llandudno, north Wales, in 1890. As a member of the Hermetic Order of the Golden Dawn, she adopted the name 'Dion Fortune'. Her interests centred on the perceived overlap between psychology, the occult and esoteric Christianity. Fortune articulated a new identity for this diverse group of enthusiasts whom she called the 'Avalonians' in contrast to the ordinary residents of Glastonbury, and her work pulls together the many strands of influence at Glastonbury at that time. Books like *Avalon of the Heart* expressed her personal esoteric vision that the pagan Tor with its sacred well and the Christian Abbey would reconcile native paganism and established Christianity.[13] The claim that Britain was one of the first nations to be converted to Christianity through the efforts of St Joseph of Arimathea bolstered the ecclesiastical influence of medieval Glastonbury. It also played a part in the Protestant Reformation narrative of British Christianity, offering a basis for *true*, i.e. not papist, Christian worship in Britain. Since the stability of English Protestantism was assured by the twentieth century, the story of Joseph and the grail offered the prospect of a new spirituality in which Glastonbury provided a model for Christianity that was Celtic as well as British. Speculation about the object from St Bride's Well and St Joseph's connection with the Abbey weaves its way through of the development of Glastonbury as a modern pilgrimage centre.

Interest in the Holy Grail had waned both in ecclesiastical and literary sources after the Reformation, but it did not disappear altogether. During the seventeenth century, the Archbishop of Armagh, James Ussher (1581–1656) referred to the Holy Grail in his Protestant history of the British Church published in 1639. Ussher's historical studies aimed to strengthen the position of the Anglican Church, and this explains his interest in the early history of Christianity in the British Isles. At first glance a reference to an object associated with the Eucharist from a fictional medieval romance is somewhat unexpected in a Protestant polemic, but for Ussher, true Christianity, brought to Britain at the dawn of the Christian era, gave hope for millennial transformation at the end of time. In *Britannicarum ecclesiarum antiquitates*, Ussher makes it clear that his sources on the 'graal' were literary. When describing the vessel used by Christ at the Passover feast, he uses terms such as *catino* and *gradalis*. His concern centred on St Joseph's apostolic mission, not the object, and his language when he mentions the Sangreal in Malory's 'fabled' *Acts of King Arthur*, is cautious about its sacramental meaning.[14] Prophecies became attached to Ussher soon after his death, and these transformed his reputation from a historian and Protestant cleric to that of millenarian prophet. At the beginning of the twentieth century, there were those who believed that Glastonbury would be the centre for a spiritual transformation of mankind, and Ussher's view of history, that the past contains the key to saving the future, appealed to such writers. Among them was Lionel Smithett Lewis, Vicar of Glastonbury, a fervent believer in its special history.

Unlike many who flocked to Glastonbury at the turn of the twentieth century, the Revd Lionel Smithett Lewis's Glastonbury was thoroughly Christian. Lewis wrote a pamphlet in defence of the legend of *St Joseph of Arimathea at Glastonbury* which went through numerous enlargements until 1955 when the last (seventh) edition appeared posthumously. Over the years, Lewis amassed what he sincerely felt was evidence for Glastonbury's claim to be the earliest Christian foundation in Britain.[15] His enthusiasm and energy were prodigious and he included all possible references to Glastonbury, Joseph and the Grail culled from chronicles, folklore and anecdotes recounted by friends and like-minded correspondents. This enthusiasm was not however matched by a clear critical judgement. He ignored the problem of late interpolations into earlier material and accepted almost any element of folklore as preserving an ancient practice. Attitudes to Glastonbury, its history and its archaeology changed dramatically over the period of thirty years between the initial pamphlet and the final edition, but Lewis's views never rose beyond the perspective on the past that he shared with his correspondents.

However, Lewis's interests reestablished the links between Glastonbury and Wales. He favoured the Nanteos cup, which was in the possession of Mrs Margaret Powell, the owner of an estate called Nanteos in Cardiganshire, over Dr Goodchild's glass bowl as the best candidate for the true Holy Grail. The colourful legend that surrounds a wooden cup once kept in a stately home in mid-Wales features escaping monks, secrets, tunnels and even a crusader. The legend begins when seven monks escaped from Glastonbury with a sacred object just as King Henry's henchmen descended on the abbey to despoil its treasures. After a perilous flight across the Welsh mountains, the monks arrived at Strata Florida Abbey in Ceredigion (now Dyfed) and were sheltered by a local family. When the last monk died, the cup was entrusted to the family who allowed sick men and women to drink from it in the hope of a miraculous cure. Over time people broke off small pieces to keep as personal relics leaving the object in its present damaged state. The cup was of course believed to be the Holy Grail. The account of the monks' escape is dramatic, as is the belief that each monk handed on responsibility for guarding the sacred cup to a companion until the last monk gave the relic into the keeping of the family that had offered them sanctuary. The reality is much more prosaic, a fourteenth-century wooden bowl from Europe, not a first-century relic from the Holy Land. The wooden cup, known as a *mazer* bowl, was probably found during the nineteenth century when it became necessary to stabilize ruins of Strata Florida Abbey, and this in turn offered an opportunity to undertake a detailed archaeological investigation. The noted archaeologist George Worthington Smith (1835–1917) made a meticulous drawing of the cup, marked with his characteristic 'WGS' monogram, and it looked then much as it does today.

Another Nanteos grail tradition became attached to a photograph of Richard Wagner. One of the owners of Nanteos, George Powell, displayed the picture in homage to a composer he admired and whom he had made a pilgrimage to Germany to meet. According to legend, however, the composer himself visited Nanteos and was so inspired by the healing cup that he wrote his opera, *Parsifal*. The same George Powell displayed the bowl as a 'healing cup' at a meeting of the Cambrian Archaeological Society in the 1870s, but by the beginning of the twentieth century, the fortunes of the family were on the wane. Mrs Margaret Powell had lost both her son and her husband to war and illness, and she began to encourage the idea that the Nanteos healing cup was actually the Holy Grail. Since then, Nanteos has changed hands several times, and the heirs of the Powell family took the object with them when they left in the 1960s.

The history of the Nanteos cup is well documented from the time it was found to its transformation into a modern Holy Grail. It was a popular local legend in the area around Nanteos, a link between the landowning families and the wider populace. The consensus reached by experts who examined the cup when it was exhibited at the National Library in Aberystwyth in the 1970s identified it as a fourteenth-century domestic vessel, a mazer bowl, made of native wych elm, not exotic olive wood.[16] Nevertheless, they were valuable objects, and a number of them survive. The lack of a metal rim may account for its poor condition, and this has given rise to yet another element in the legend, the belief that pilgrims bit off relics and caused extensive damage. Occasional dramatic stories about the 'Welsh Holy Grail' still appear in newspaper accounts, and the advent of the

Internet has brought this charming, but minor, archaeological find to the attention of a wider audience.[17]

An alternative tradition identifies the Nanteos cup as a healing vessel made from the wood of the True Cross and claims that is was an object of veneration at the medieval abbey of Strata Florida, rather than Glastonbury.[18] These are typical themes in legend narratives about the survival of an ancient object. Dramatic and miraculous events, like Joseph's legendary journey to Glastonbury and the subsequent flight of the monks to Wales, explain the appearance of the Nanteos cup in an unexpected place. A perceived catastrophe, the plundering of religious sites by Henry VIII, threatens the existence of this sacred object, but someone recognises its true worth, rescues it, and preserves it in secret. Finally the object reappears, carrying with it – and transmitting to those who accept its reality – some of the beneficial qualities of the past.

A pamphlet on the Nanteos Cup appeared a few years before Goodchild's bowl was discovered at Bride's Well, but it was not until the 1930s that Lewis contacted the owner, Mrs Powell, about her 'grail'. As part of his attempts to convince Mrs Powell to 'return' the 'grail' to Glastonbury, he gave her a copy of Archbishop Ussher's prophecies, which is the most likely source for yet another tradition attached to the Nanteos cup, that 'the church shall claim its own'. He also put her in touch with Sir William Crookes, glass specialist and psychical expert, who examined Tudor Pole's glass bowl. He urged her to return the Cup to Glastonbury and to stop lending it to the sick whose reported tendency to take souvenirs was, he felt, destroying a precious relic. Lewis's requests fell on deaf ears, and Mrs Powell decided to keep her cup at Nanteos. However the Vicar of Glastonbury has left his mark on its traditions. In the later 1920s he initiated the custom of sending a sprig from the Glastonbury thorn to the reigning British monarch, thereby adding a royal touch to the legend that Joseph of Arimathea planted his staff in the ground on Wearyall Hill. The Holy Thorn has bloomed in Glastonbury ever since, despite attempts to destroy it, and is often cited as proof of the antiquity of the Joseph legend. Like so many legends the ceremonies and traditions attached to the thorn are not as ancient as they seem, but reflect the continued response to Glastonbury's ever-changing spiritual landscape.[19]

Many artists and literary figures were attracted to Glastonbury. Among them was the poet and translator, Sebastian Evans (1823–1908) who translated the work of Geoffrey of Monmouth and wrote a book on the meaning of the grail. Most crucially for the development of the grail legend, his translation of *Perlesvaus*, under the title the *High History of the Holy Grail*, made this French romance available for an English reading public for the first time.[20] While working on illustrations inspired by Sebastian Evans's translation in the summer of 1929, the artist and theosophist Katherine Maltwood had a sudden insight that Glastonbury itself was the subject of the grail story. She believed that the *Perlesvaus* romance contained a coded description of a secret landscape. She projected the Grail story so completely onto the physical landscape of Glastonbury that she believed an ancient Zodiac was imprinted on the land. Although she never made it clear who constructed these zodiacal figures, she implied that they were a spontaneous creation of the sacredness of Glastonbury itself.[21]

The Anglo-Welsh writer John Cowper Powys (1872–1963) returned from America after the First World War to live first in southwest England and then in Wales. He described Somerset as 'shifty wavering undulating fluctuating country full of Phantoms … by far the most enchanted ground in England',[22] and he popularised the idea of Glastonbury as the legendary Isle of Avalon, home of the Holy Grail. In his novel A *Glastonbury Romance* (1932) John Cowper Powys, through the mystic-cum-antiquarian hero of his novel, characterized the grail 'a fragment of the absolute known in those parts for five thousand years as a cauldron, a horn, a krater, a mwys, a well, a kernos, a platter, a cup and even a nameless stone'.[23] Although the novel belongs to the world of mystic visionaries who oppose the forces of industrialization, Powys himself had an exceptionally wide-ranging knowledge of the subject, and his description lists names for the grail and theories about its origin at the time the novel was written.

That St Joseph of Arimathea ever carried the grail along the road to Glastonbury is frankly unlikely. The legend that he took the Holy Grail westwards was in circulation by the end of the twelfth century, and within a hundred years, the prose romances of the *Vulgate Cycle* described how Joseph collected the blood that flowed from Christ's wounds in a vessel known as the grail and how he and his family escaped to become the guardians of the sacred object. Medieval writers at Glastonbury Abbey incorporated the St Joseph legend into its history, but the Holy Grail itself was largely omitted as belonging to fiction. Eventually, chronicle sources combined Joseph, the grail bearer in the romances, with traditions about St Joseph at Glastonbury into one legend, namely that Joseph possessed two vessels, one containing the blood, the other the sweat of Christ. This transformed the grail into a more acceptable relic linked to the Holy Blood, but its real impact was felt later. John Cowper Powys called the grail a 'magnet gatherer of all that came to Glastonbury'.[24] The idea of the grail as a psychic force that would attract both pagans and Christians was very much in tune with what was happening in Glastonbury at the time and has continued to the present day.

SECRET GRAILS AND HIDDEN MESSAGES

THE GRAIL HAS HAD a complex history since its appearance in Chrétien de Troyes's medieval verse romance. Its importance as a literary motif diminished as other literary fashions eclipsed the romance genre, and religious reform also weakened its impact. However, its fortunes rose once more in the context of romantic nineteenth-century reinterpretations of the past, and the revival of interest in medieval Arthurian tradition. Until the beginning of the twentieth century Glastonbury was a small intimate world; today it is a magnet for grail seekers. At the same time that Glastonbury's role as part of the modern grail legend was expanding, a similar alternative view of the grail developed in France, centred not on St Joseph of Arimathea but on the Templars, an order of warrior knights founded in the twelfth century and disbanded two centuries later.

Rumours that the Order of the Knights Templar survived in secret laid the foundation for another interpretation of the grail, the belief that it was the centre of a vast conspiracy, and the Templars soon began to rival the Celts as a popular source for the grail story. In order to create a secret history, the modern Templar myth reinterpreted episodes of the grail romances as actual historical events, and today, the myth of the Templars and the grail is sustained by books, media coverage and an ever-expanding network of Internet sites.[1] This secret conspiracy was satirized in a novel *Foucault's Pendulum*, by the Italian author, Umberto Eco in which a group of scholars create a fictional conspiracy whose central principle is that 'the Templars are involved in absolutely everything'. This mixture of speculation and outright fiction about conspiracies, Templar secrets and the grail became even more widely known with the publication of the best-selling conspiracy thriller, *The Da Vinci Code* at the beginning of the twenty-first century.[2]

'The Poor Knights of Christ of the Temple which is in Jerusalem', commonly referred to as the Templars, was founded at the beginning of the twelfth century. The Order was based at the church of the Holy Sepulchre in Jerusalem, but moved to the site known to Christians as Solomon's Temple. At first it struggled to attract members, and the circumstances of its founding were not recorded until later. These later accounts attempt to make sense of fragmented, and sometimes inconsistent, material relating to the uncertain start of what became a major institution in Europe. Despite the fact that a number of excellent histories present an authoritative picture of the origin, development and legacy of the Order,[3] popular writers continue to search for clues about hidden meanings, with the result that sources have been over-interpreted to imply a level of secrecy and conspiracy that did not exist. After its uncertain start, membership and donations increased and the pious knights who were attracted to the Order soon adopted the familiar habit with a red cross on a white mantle. An important aspect of the Templar way of life was the protection of pilgrims in the Holy Land. The European holdings were divided into provinces whose role was to raise money for this project. Consequently, the Templars became involved in agriculture, trade, money and, inevitably, politics. The Master and his officials were based at the eastern fortress headquarters at Acre, but there were other fortresses scattered across Europe and the Holy Land. These fortresses represented a huge investment of money, manpower and prestige and their loss, culminating in the fall of Acre in 1291, was a crushing financial and psychological blow. After Jacques de Molay was elected Master of the Order of the Temple in 1293, he travelled to Europe to gather support for a crusade to reconquer the Holy Land. Unfortunately, the political situation did not favour this venture, and the result was disastrous. King Philip IV, whose handsome appearance earned him the name of the Fair (*le Bel*), had strengthened the power of the French monarchy through clever politics and sheer force of will. The election of a French cleric as Pope Clement V increased his influence, and this was further strengthened when the papacy transferred to Avignon in France. In October 1307, Philip IV ordered the arrest of the French Templars on charges of heresy, blasphemy and eventually sorcery. Pope Clement V was initially reluctant, but he eventually ordered the arrest and inter-rogation of the Templars. Through his political power and his influ-ence over the pope, Philip IV was instrumental in having the Order disbanded in 1311. As a consequence, Philip and Clement figure as villains-in-chief in the modern grail myth of the destruction of the Knights Templar.

Popular explanations for the charges brought against the Templars favour secret wisdom and conspiracy, but in truth these charges were more a matter of political expediency. Heresy and blasphemy were a serious matter, but sorcery was a newer element in the pattern of accusation. Anecdotes involving obscene kissing, black cats, secret night meetings and the worship of demonic idols have become famil-iar in accounts of European witch hunts, but accusations of sorcery could also be used to undermine political rivals, which is exactly what Philip IV intended. The accusation that the Templars worshipped an idol called Bahomat, a variant of the name Mohammed, also reflects anti-Islamic stereotypes. Such practices were fictions of prejudice, since Islam forbids the worship of idols, but the accusation implied that, instead of defending Christendom, the Templars had adopted Muslim practice. There were doubts about the charges, especially outside the French sphere of influence, and some contemporary com-mentators were aware that torture played a role in confessions, but the accumulation of scandal and accusation eventually resulted in the suppression of the Order.[4]

Besides idolatry, the Templars were accused of wearing secret amulets, spitting or trampling the Cross and performing unnatural acts, and the ceremony of investiture into the Order also featured in the accusations. The Templar investiture was similar to the one used for investing a new knight, namely a dawn ceremony after an all-night vigil. It was usually private, but it was certainly not a secret initiation rite. Despite this, some commentators maintain that a secret rite existed even though no trace of one was ever found. The round naves of some Templar churches, such as the most famous example in the New Temple in London are another focus for speculation. The round naves provided a visual link to the Church of the Holy Sepulchre in Jerusalem, but much has been made of hidden codes in Templar architecture and the possibility that Templar ships conducted global exploration. Although not all Templars were fighting knights, there is no evidence for a specialized class of Templar masons or architects who could build churches with complex symbolic geometry.

Alternative theories about the Templars and their beliefs focus on the period before their official recognition. Details regarding the origins of the Order vary, but none of the medieval documents suggest that the founder members were anything other than pious orthodox believers. At the time of the Crusades, the Temple Mount, now the Al Aqsa Mosque, was thought to be the site of Solomon's Temple, although there is no concrete evidence of such an ancient building. The writings of the founders of the Order, men like Hugh de Payns, show no trace of the esoteric philosophy that allegedly motivated the secret searches so important in modern Templar myths. For the Templars, faith was a straightforward matter. They were not a learned Order, indeed quite the reverse, and one of the striking differences between the Templars and the non-military monastic Orders like the Cistercians was the lack of theological education. Instead of an interval during which the Order struggled to establish itself, which is the explanation suggested by the historical records, alternative authors see a period of covert activity during which a secret cabal looked for powerful talismans, among them the Holy Grail. Early records only appear mysterious if one presupposes there has been a deliberate attempt to hide secret activities. Despite this, the assumption that lack of evidence is itself evidence of a conspiracy remains an essential part of modern grail legends like the Templar myth.

The sites of several Templar foundations have been excavated, and the archaeology provides additional information about daily life and economic activity. European archives preserve documents recording the Order's activities, and although material has certainly been lost, there is no indication that records containing esoteric secrets were deliberately destroyed. None of these sources contain information about belief, and this is what many modern readers familiar with myths about Templar treasure and esotericism wish to know. Despite the absence of evidence that the Order was involved in intellectual or esoteric pursuits, modern grail legends hint that this was somehow its real function, and that the Templars went underground to continue their mysterious activities even after the Order was disbanded. Ironically, in this odd looking-glass world of secrets and conspiracies, it is lack of evidence that fuels conspiracy thinking and the more firmly convinced certain writers become that there must be hidden secrets somewhere.

By the nineteenth century, the Templars were viewed in a more favourable light as a group who rebelled against tyranny and repression. Nostalgia for a world of chivalry made it fashionable to theorize about deep meanings concealed within the adventures of medieval romance. The Order also became identified with the Cathars, a religious sect based in southern France and branded as heretics during the Middle Ages. The very fact of persecution allowed both Templars and Cathars to be seen as martyred members of secret societies. The two groups became linked, as they never were historically, by loose notions of alternative Christianity and ancient wisdom. Such fictitious links are invoked to explain perceived geometrical patterns and occult meanings in paintings and in the landscapes of France, Scotland and elsewhere. Such ideas seem naïve, but the conviction that a secret system is concealed in the beliefs of long-repressed organizations has become a powerful tool of alternative history. The assumptions and speculations that underpin the alleged secrets of the Cathars and Templars are connected by a common thread, and that thread is the grail.

The rise of Freemasonry in the eighteenth century provided another context for nostalgic reconstruction. Freemasonry epitomised important values of eighteenth-century society, such as a strong work ethic, social tolerance and the application of rational principles to scientific study and the understanding of religion. There was however a contrasting interest in secret meanings, mystical speculation and elaborate ritual. Members of Masonic lodges were usually professional men, part of a rising middle class whose influence was changing the political and social world of Europe. Not surprisingly such social and intellectual innovation provoked a reaction, a desire to return to a stable past or to access an alternative knowledge capable of transforming the future. This created a climate in which speculation about secret societies could flourish. One of the dominant attitudes to religion at this time, certainly the one most prominent among the intelligentsia, is summed up in the idea that human reason was sufficient to observe and to understand the divine plan in the natural world. This approach stood in sharp contrast to the complex theology and rituals by which an elite controlled access to divine benefit. This rational approach to religion also provoked a counter movement, one that sought deeper realities behind the confusing array of experience and looked for hidden connections, apparent to the initiated, that could transform society.

Freemasonry absorbed legends about King Solomon's Temple and the masons who built it and used them as metaphors for its own origin and organisation. A more speculative strain within Freemasonry however interpreted these legends as a literal reflection of Masonic history. The name of the Templars and the fact that they occupied a section of the Temple Mount in Jerusalem, the traditional location of Solomon's temple, provided an opportunity for the mythic history of the two organizations to be combined. This gave rise to yet another speculation, namely that the foundation myth of Freemasonry might also be connected to the Templars.[5]

One of the first to make the connection between the crusading orders as guardians of secret doctrines and Freemasonry was a Catholic convert who adopted the name Chevalier Andrew Michael Ramsey (c.1687–1743). He wrote a book in the spirit of the gothic novel, full of parchments in hollow pillars and secret chambers under Solomon's Temple, just exactly the motifs so crucial to later grail legends like those associated with Rennes-le-Château, Shugborough and Rosslyn Chapel. Another revision of Templar history suggested that Jacques de Molay, the last Grand Master, secretly removed a vast treasure before his execution and concealed it in hollow pillars at a Templar site. The idea that treasure was hidden from King Philip of France has proved a tenacious motif in modern legends, especially in France. Yet another revivalist, George Frederick Johnson, a self-styled Scottish nobleman, suggested that the escaping Templars had fled to Scotland. The Masonic myth of Hiram, the murdered architect of Solomon's temple, became fused with the execution of de Molay, forming yet another strand of legend in the traditions surrounding the so-called Apprentice Pillar in Rosslyn Chapel.

A sinister political dimension was added to the supposed occult conspiracy by linking the Templars to the disgraced Illuminati, a group of radical intellectuals based in Bohemia in the late eighteenth century. This encouraged occult tales about shadowy Grand Masters orchestrating plots to overthrow heads of state. For example, Abbé Augustin Barruel (1797) depicted both Templars and Freemasons as revolutionaries trying to destabilise European monarchies and the Catholic Church. For Barruel, everything was connected in a vast historical conspiracy of evil, and this world-view introduced rumours about a sinister political plot into the Templar myth. Another conspiracy mythologist, Joseph von Hammer-Purgstall transformed the Templars into pagan idol-worshippers, and here finally, the Holy Grail becomes part of the legend. In *The Mystery of Bahomat Revealed* (1818), Hammer-Purgstall equated Wolfram von Eschenbach's *templeisen*, the guardians of the grail in the medieval German romance *Parzival*, with the Knights Templar and transformed the grail into a secret symbol with no Christian links. He saw these dubious Templar 'grails' on any number of ancient monuments unrecorded outside the pages of his own work, but Hammer-Purgstall set a precedent for reading secret meaning into iconography that would be taken up with enthusiasm by later grail seekers.

Medieval romance writers did not equate the Templars with the Grail knights, and, at best, Wolfram's reference to *templeisen* is ambiguous. As neo-templar and masonic organisations took root however, a different view of the Order emerged. Cathars and Templars were transformed from conspirators themselves to the target of yet another conspiracy. This one aimed to suppress the secret knowledge of independent thinkers, such as Cathars and Templars, who struggled against the tyranny of an oppressive church and state. One of the symbols of this struggle became a secret grail, the embodiment of alternative wisdom, part of an alternative Christian world or a remnant of benevolent paganism. This modern myth-making not only transformed Wolfram's *templeisen* into Templars, but Wolfram's fictional source, the Provençal poet Kyout, provided a means to link the Templars with another medieval sect, the Cathars. The Templars were involved in the crusades in the Holy Land, while the Cathars, or Albigensians as they are also called, were the target of an internal crusade against a supposed heretical sect within Europe itself. They too have become part of the modern grail legend.[6]

The crusade against the Cathars began in 1208 with the murder of the papal legate by someone in the entourage of the Count of Toulouse. This brought the tensions between the Catholic Church and the Cathars of southern France to breaking point. These tensions were as much political as religious, since the powerful Counts of Toulouse in the Languedoc region of France threatened the influence of the French monarchy. The Latin Christian church regarded Cathar beliefs as heretical, but the sect preached openly and its influence was strong, especially in the Albi region of southern France (hence the alternative name Albigensians). It was a public not a secret sect with a coherent doctrine and structure, and Cathar records document the existence of a flourishing and dynamic cult. The Cathars were critical of the sacraments of the church, which they considered corrupt. There were no priests, but a class of holy men and women (*perfecti*), who committed themselves to an ascetic lifestyle, acted as teachers, and provided a focus for Cathar life. Their doctrines recognized two divine principles, one a perfect and eternal god who created all things spiritual, the other a demonic principle who created the material world. Cathar explanations for the origin of the material world invoked the myth of Lucifer's fall and a belief that angels of light who had fallen with Lucifer were trapped in material bodies. God and the material world were completely separate, and matter itself was viewed as transitory and corrupt.

The executions of Cathar leaders during the Albigensian Crusade presented a spectacle of committed men and women going willingly to die under the stigma of heresy. Only in retrospect were they seen as victims of a repressive regime. This view was reinforced by events during the siege at Montségur, whose destruction spawned tales of secret treasure. The fortress of Montségur occupied a rocky prominence in the Languedoc. Before the final siege in 1243, many Cathars took refuge there, and, just before the surrender, a few escaped under cover of darkness. Their fate is not known, but it has become the basis for speculations that they secretly took the Holy Grail with them. Cathar records make no mention of such an object, and since their beliefs rejected the orthodox Christian sacraments, the grail with its overtones of the Eucharist sacrament would not fit easily into Cathar beliefs.[7]

In the context of the Templar myth, the supposed mystery of Montségur has provided a platform for a heady mixture of esoteric and political ideas. France had its romantic revivalists similar to those at Glastonbury. Both groups shared an interest in esotericism and secret messages, but the French revivalists were generally more political. From the end of the nineteenth to the middle of the twentieth centuries, French writers such as Deodat Roché and Josephin Péladan, and the German Otto Rahn created an imaginary world of Templars, Cathars, secrets and grails embedded in the landscape of the French Languedoc. At the end of the twentieth century, the small town of Rennes-le-Château became a focus for similar speculations. The path that led there involved grail romances and Templar legends, as well as a painting by a famous French Baroque artist, Nicholas Poussin, in which Arcadian shepherds gaze at a classical tomb inscribed with the Latin phrase 'Et in Arcadia ego'. The story of Rennes-le-Château took the idea of an alternative reality onto another level.

Although none of the grail romances have direct links with southern France, Kyout, Wolfram von Eschenbach's fictional source for his romance *Parzival*, was identified with the medieval poet, Guiot de Provence. There is no evidence that Guiot ever wrote verse romances, much less that he had esoteric leanings. Nevertheless, the identification linked this important German grail romance to the Cathar myth. For French writers, the culture of the Languedoc region embodied a spirit of independent resistance, and a possible link between historical events in southern France and Wolfram's masterpiece opened new possibilities for secret discoveries.

At the beginning of the twentieth century, two French civil servants, Deodat Roché, and Joséphin Péladan linked Cathars and Templars as custodians of an esoteric secret, and they suggested that this secret was entwined in some mystical way with the national character of France. Deodat Roché founded a society aimed at reviving these secret Cathar doctrines, while Joséphin Péladan identified

Munsalveasche, the grail castle in Wolfram's poem with the Cathar stronghold of Montségur. Like so many revivals, they avoid the difficulties of historical accuracy by invoking conspiracies, and their mythology teems with strange documents in pillars, mysterious tombs, ciphers and riddles.[8] By the time Otto Rahn, a German explorer who worked for Heinrich Himmler, visited southern France in the 1930s, Cathar mythology was well established, and Rahn had little difficulty in identifying the romanticised Cathars with the Templars and placing them in the context of a his own brand of Teutonic mythology. Rahn was influenced by the work of French writers like Péladan, whom he knew from contact with occult circles in Paris. His first book *The Crusade Against the Grail* (*Kreuzzuge gegen den Graal*) in 1933 expanded the parallels between the Albigensian crusade and Wolfram's romance. Rahn identified characters in Wolfram's *Parzival* romance – such as the grail maiden, the Grail King, the hermit, and even the hero, Parzival himself – with historical Cathar figures. Such identifications were impossible to substantiate, but the undaunted Rahn went even further. In his version the 'grail maiden' presided over the sacred precinct of the grail, namely Montségur, and just before it fell, Cathars, who were really Templars, escaped with the grail.[9]

Rahn believed that an ancient pre-Christian Cathar cult was embedded in the Languedoc and formed part of a much wider Germanic mythological world. The Teutonic nationalism which permeated his fantasy is even stronger in his second book. *Lucifer's Courtiers* (*Luzifers Hofgesind*, 1937) drew, loosely, on a Cathar belief that angels of light were trapped in the material world created by the fallen Lucifer. However, Rahn re-interpreted this into a cosmology in which Lucifer was the real deity at the centre of an ancient untainted religion pitted against the Judaic god of the Old Testament. Rahn's sympathy for Nazi ideas was an important factor in the spin he put on this interpretation. However, he himself fell out of favour, probably because of rumours of homosexuality, and was found frozen to death on a mountainside in Austria, an apparent suicide. Perhaps it is not surprising that Otto Rahn's death, with its overtones of Nazi occultism and homosexuality, has become the focus of conspiracy rumours, specifically that Rahn was sent to the Languedoc on a special mission for Himmler himself to find the grail and bring it back to Nazi Germany.

His story has influenced a stream of alternative history and fiction about Hitler's alleged search for objects of power like the grail.[10] Accounts of arcane rituals in Nazi Germany have found their way into Dennis Wheatley's occult novel, *They Used Dark Forces* and Duncan Kyle's spy thriller, *Black Camelot*,[11] and of course Nazi villains compete with Indiana Jones and his father for possession of the grail in Steven Spielberg's *Indiana Jones and the Last Crusade*.[12]

Traditions about secret and hidden grails in France added conservative political overtones to speculations about Templar secrets and Cathar mysticism. Although broadly contemporary with developments at Glastonbury, the French grail movement was more fragmented and the grail revival in France might have stayed on the fringes of French popular culture except for an alternative history that became an overnight publishing sensation.

RENNES-LE-CHÂTEAU

One of the most widely known modern interpretations of the grail legend first appeared as a series of documentaries on British television. The book that followed, *The Holy Blood and the Holy Grail*, became a best-seller. Both the argument of the book and the research on which it was based have been extensively criticised, but it continues to influence the conspiracy genre in publishing and on the Internet. It has also influenced fiction, notably Dan Brown's detective thriller, *The Da Vinci Code*, and the sophisticated satire of Umberto Eco's *Foucault's Pendulum*. Several updates and sequels have followed the original publication, although the controversy peaked somewhat after the release of a Hollywood film based on the book in 2006 and an unsuccessful action for alleged copyright infringement.[13]

The crux of the argument is that the Holy Grail is not a physical object, but a person, the descendant of a sacred bloodline, and the medieval grail, the *sangreal*, is a misunderstanding of the phrase *sang real* or *royal (holy) blood*. The confusion between *san greal* (grail) and *sang real* (blood) goes back to the English writer John Hardyng in the fifteenth century,[14] but the authors of the twentieth-century book go further and claim that Jesus Christ was not divine. In addition he had children by his wife, Mary Magdalene who escaped to southern France where their offspring married into a noble family. This family became the Merovingian dynasty, the first Christian kings of France. By the time Charlemagne was crowned in 800, however, the Merovingian line had died out. In the tenth century, Hugh Capet became the first king of the Capetian dynasty, followed by the Bourbon dynasty, which remained in power until the French Revolution and was restored briefly in the nineteenth century. The startling and controversial thesis put forward by the authors of *The Holy Blood and the Holy Grail* was based on a French treasure story about the activities of a nineteenth-century priest at Rennes-le-Château, a small town in southern France. According to this story, the priest, Bérenger Saunière, found mysterious documents in an ancient column whose content was so shocking that the authorities paid him to keep the information quiet. When these documents were finally decoded, they revealed the identity of the last descendant of this divine royal bloodline.[15]

This alternative reading of history asserts that the divine bloodline of the Merovingian kings did not die out. Mainstream Christianity attempted to destroy their descendants in order to maintain papal power and influence, but a secret organisation known as the Priory of Sion, founded during the Crusades, protected the divine bloodline. The Order of the Knights Templar was created to give military and financial support to the Priory. According to a tradition about the siege of Montségur, one of the Cathar defenders interrogated by the Inquisition claimed that a treasure had been removed the night before the citadel fell. The recorded account strongly suggests that the 'treasure' was monetary, but subsequent attempts to recast the Cathars as a secret organisation have insisted that the mysterious treasure smuggled out of Montségur by the medieval Cathars was the real truth about the grail. After the suppression of the Cathars, the Priory allied itself with Freemasons and other secret societies to ensure the survival of the 'real' meaning of the grail. Despite books, television documentaries and Internet sites arguing both sides of this theory, the historical evidence does not offer much support for an ancient mystery at Rennes-le-Château.[16] Rumours about local eccentrics, treasure, mysterious artefacts and secrets provide the basis for many local legends. They add colour and charm to familiar, even rather ordinary, sites and provide an imaginative synthesis in which events are never random.

Bérenger Saunière was appointed to the parish church of Rennes-le-Château, a small town in the Languedoc, in 1885, but the first account of treasure appeared much later, after Saunière's property had become a hotel. A French journalist published a pamphlet with details about hidden manuscripts, mysterious buildings and clues hidden in a famous painting. According to this report, the priest found documents inside a pillar while restoring the dilapidated church. The original documents have been conveniently lost and only survive as modern typed 'transcriptions'. The key to the mystery lies in a painting by the famous seventeenth-century French artist, Nicolas Poussin, whose Les Bergers d'Arcadie depict Arcadian shepherds gazing at the tomb inscribed with the words 'Et in Arcadia ego' (Even in Arcadia [am] I). The painting supposedly reflects an actual tomb in the countryside near Rennes-le-Château whose secrets are revealed when a complex geometric grid is superimposed on the painting. After this 'discovery', Saunière became very prosperous, undertook elaborate renovations to the church and built a mysterious tower, all of which have been interpreted as evidence of secret Cathar and Templar beliefs. Saunière died in poverty in 1917, but his housekeeper continued to live in the priest's house. She regaled the new owner with tales of secret treasure, but she had a stroke and died with the secret, if there ever was one, intact.

This is very much a 'what if' approach to events, asking readers to consider that seeming coincidences in an otherwise pedestrian story have a deeper significance that will lead us into a world of extraordinary events and cosmic conspiracies.[17] A less dramatic account of events suggests that rumours about treasure and the priest's wealth were exaggerated. Saunière's royalist sympathies for the old French monarchy, rather than an interest in the occult, brought him to the attention of the authorities, while the elaborate church decorations were in keeping with late nineteenth-century taste and have parallels elsewhere. Nothing in the typescript documents 'found' in the pillar can be dated convincingly, and Poussin painted an imaginary tomb, not an actual structure in the countryside around Rennes-le-Château.[18]

Nevertheless, a group of French amateur antiquarians adapted elements from this extraordinary local legend to create the Priory of Sion (Prieuré de Sion) in 1956. According to 'Les Dossiers Secret', Bérenger Saunière's secret code plus clues in Poussin's painting of Arcadian shepherds revealed the existence of the lost Merovingian heir to the French throne, a descendant of the line of Clovis, the first Christian king of France. The protection of this heir had been entrusted to the Priory of Sion, and a succession of distinguished intellectuals and artists that included Nicholas Poussin had been grand masters of this secret organisation. This fictional history went back to the earliest roots of French culture, and happily swept aside the French Revolution, and the dynasties of Bourbon and Capetian kings to set itself in a time before Charlemagne.

The contrast between the utopian pastoral world of Arcadia and the knowledge that even here death is inevitable was a powerful image in art and literature, and Nicholas Poussin painted the subject more than once. However, the inscribed tomb in *Shepherds Gazing at a Tomb in Arcadia* became a pivot for the Rennes mystery. Hidden geometry supposedly linked the inscribed tomb in the painting with the actual landscape around Rennes-le-Château, although there is no record of such a 'tomb' structure at the time Poussin painted his vision of Arcadia in the seventeenth century. There are no hints in Poussin's writings that he had any leanings towards codes and secret messages. In the context of the classical imagery that pervaded the artist's work, the existence of a tomb in the pastoral world of Arcadia reflects a stoic attitude to life's uncertainty.[19] The 'Dossiers Secret', however, present a different interpretation, namely that this painting contains a secret available only to the initiated who understand the code.

The Priory of Sion reflects the spirit of other esoteric interpretations of the grail, but the motivation behind its creation is unclear. Different researchers suggest everything from surrealistic role-playing to right-wing politics, or just that the authors of *Holy Blood* took the French treasure story too literally. The founding members were not concerned with theology or even with the grail as such, but the secret cabal they created echoed earlier theories that historicized the grail romances in France. The original Priory was concerned with a secret heir from a long lost dynasty, but for the authors of *Holy Blood*

Holy Grail in the 1970s, the story was altogether more grandiose. For them, the Priory protected the actual descendants of Christ and Mary Magdalene, and the accusations made against Cathars and Templars were transformed into a conspiracy to eradicate the hereditary succession of a human Christ and his wife in order to maintain the power of the Roman papacy. Soon after the book appeared, the idea of an alternative, and of course suppressed, form of Christianity became linked to another popular conspiracy theme, namely the search for the divine feminine. This added another dimension to the secret, namely that the medieval veneration of Mary Magdalene concealed the remnants of an ancient cult devoted to a pre-Christian goddess, remnants of which could still be found in southern France.[20] What was originally a local organisation has become the centrepiece of pseudo-historical books on alternative Christianity, theories about the Holy Grail, and mass-market fiction.

At first glance, the *Holy Blood* book presents a complex theory built on an enormous array of facts supported by a vast bibliography. It is partly that which makes it so attractive. Direct descendants of this bloodline, the Merovingian dynasty who ruled France from the fifth to the eighth centuries have been protected through the ages by the Cathars, Templars and, most crucially, by an organisation known as the Priory of Sion. All have been targeted by the power structures of church and state. In the world of conspiracy thinking, this antagonism was a sustained campaign to counter an alternative religion practiced in secret and passed from one set of guardians to another. Since the theory focuses on conspiracies and codes rather than the practicalities of doctrine, the exact nature of this alternative Christianity is somewhat vague, but the notion of an hereditary sacred bloodline has given rise to an extremely productive modern grail legend.

The aim of the esoteric and occult approach in any case is not really history, but a search for a principle that will unify diverse aspects of mythology, literature and culture. Despite the book's popularity, it did not garner much critical acclaim. The controversy did not hurt sales, but neither did the 'shocking revelations' produce any observable effects on world history. Television documentaries, exposé books and the testimony of several founding members have revealed the largely fictional sources for the Rennes-le-Château mystery, but the legend lives on. The claims of *Holy Blood Holy Grail* surfaced again in the wake of Dan Brown's immensely successful *The Da Vinci Code*, the second in a trilogy of conspiracy thrillers published in 2003. Earlier French revivalists like Maurice Magre and Joseph Péladan had explored links between the grail and the Cathar crusade in their novels, but Dan Brown, already a successful novelist specializing in conspiracy thrillers, incorporated these alternative ideas about the grail into a best-selling book. Brown's preface suggested a degree of historical authority for the rituals and institutions mentioned in the book. While medieval authors, like Chrétien de Troyes and Wolfram von Eschenbach, used such conceits for literary effect, many of Brown's readers took his novel literally. The emphasis in the novel is on action rather than character. The plot combines alternative themes about a covert Christian sect, speculative ideas about the New Testament, popular myths about Templars and Cathars, hidden treasure legends, conspiracy rumours and vague esoteric ideas which had become popular with the rise of new age spirituality. The material was, however, repackaged in an inventive way. Certain religious groups reacted against the book's message, and a raft of handbooks, web blogs and television documentaries followed.[21]

THE SHEPHERD'S MONUMENT AT SHUGBOROUGH

The grail as secret history is a very adaptable legend, and traditions attached to an eighteenth-century monument standing in the gardens of the Shugborough Estate in Staffordshire illustrate this point very well. The monument has a carved relief of Nicolas Poussin's Arcadian shepherds gazing at a tomb inscribed with the words 'Et in Arcadia ego'. Beneath this is a cipher of ten letters: D.O.U.O.S.V.A.V.V.M. These letters and the fact that the carving is a mirror image of the original painting have attracted the attention of cryptologists and grail hunters. The monument at Shugborough had no connections with medieval grail legends. It reflected the intellectual interests of an eighteenth-century family who admired classical culture and the Arcadian symbolism that Poussin immortalized in art. However, this painting is central to the Rennes-le-Château mystery, and the authors of *Holy Blood and Holy Grail* extended their speculations to include the monument at Shugborough with its seemingly mysterious cipher. Since then a location with no prior links to Templars, medieval romance or the grail has been absorbed into a dynamic modern legend. In 2005 two code-breakers, who worked at Bletchley Park during the Second World War, suggested new solutions for the meaning of the inscription and for a time at least the estate website enabled visitors to engage in the endeavour of finding secret codes.[22]

The Ansons who owned Shugborough were a sophisticated and erudite eighteenth-century family with an interest in classical culture, especially the philosophy of stoicism. This philosophy stressed that life and its blessing were transitory, and Arcadia was a favourite metaphor for the transience of life. The words 'Et in Arcadia ego' (even in Arcadia [am] I), an ambiguous reference to death in the midst of life, encapsulate the fashionable stoic beliefs of eighteenth-century classicism. However, some observers have read secret meanings into the fact that the carving of Poussin's shepherds at Shugborough is reversed and that the proportions differ from the original painting. The explanation for this is quite straightforward. The engraving which the carver copied was reversed in printing, and the rectangular shape of the original landscape painting had to be compressed into a vertical space. Thus pragmatic considerations, rather than esoteric concerns, account for the distortions in the arrangement of the figures.

The ten letters below the carving are separated by full stops, the usual practice for abbreviations for words, which suggests that this is a cipher rather than a code. Among the proposed solutions for the inscription is one attributed to an 'unnamed code breaker' occupying a senior position in some unspecified intelligence network who used a series of code-grids to produce a phrase, *Jesus H Defy*. As it stands, this has no more inherent sense than the original series of letters. In order to get a more satisfactory solution, the code-breaker invoked the Priory of Sion version of the Templar myth with its supposed secret doctrine revealing that Christ was human. 'H' was identified with the Greek letter X (chi χ) and equated with '*messiah*' or '*Christ*' which was translated as 'deity', and the phrase was re-interpreted as *Jesus (the Deity) Defy*. However, the Greek letter 'H' (eta) consistently refers to the letter 'e' in the name Jesus, as in the abbreviation IHS, the first three letters of the name in Greek. The words *messiah* and *Christ* mean 'the anointed one' not 'deity'. Such speculations depend on the supposed unorthodox views of romanticised Templars, but code-breaking grids, an unknown code breaker 'high up' in some intelligence network, the Templars, and the secret Priory at Rennes are the elements that make the contemporary grail legend so compelling. Unfortunately they are also the elements which, to say the least, represent an over-interpretation of the imagery and letters on this monument and take this explanation so unequivocally into the world of modern legend.

The Anson family and the intellectual world of the eighteenth century provide a more coherent explanation for the meaning of this monument. Admiral George Anson and his wife, Lady Elizabeth Yorke, lived on the Shugborough estate owned by his brother, Thomas. George Anson's wife, Elizabeth, described Shugborough as 'Arcady' and addressed her brother-in law, Thomas, as *Gentil Berger* (Shepherd). The talented Elizabeth Anson even copied an earlier version of Nicholas Poussin's Arcadia painting, and there is a portrait of her holding her drawing. A poem entitled 'An Emblematical Basso Relievo after a famous picture of Nicolas Poussin', preserved among the family papers, mentions the monument and its inscription. It refers to Arcadia and to 'life's fleeting moments [that] gently steal away'. The image of a tomb in Arcadia recalls descriptions of pastoral bliss in Virgil's *Eclogues*. The phrase 'Et in Arcadia ego' implies both the transience of life – 'even in Arcadia am I [i.e. Death]' – and the beauty of eternity – 'I [the occupant of the tomb] am in Arcadia'. The contrast in *Les Bergers D'Arcadie* between the pastoral scene and the tomb suggests the clever ambiguities that appealed to sophisticated painters like Poussin and educated patrons with an interest in classical art and culture like the Anson family.

The family poem of 1758 alludes to the Poussin *bas relief* on the monument at Shugborough, but there is nothing about a cipher until 1767. During that period both Lady Elizabeth and her husband had died. The cipher therefore, may commemorate the affection between Elizabeth (the wife and sister) and her husband George (the widower) who survived her by only a few years. Alternatively, it could be a memorial to the parents of George and Thomas Anson, or even to someone close to Thomas Anson himself. The first and last letters of the cipher, D. M., are a Roman funerary abbreviation for the phrase *Diis Manibus* (To the Souls of the Departed). The remaining letters could stand for the Latin phrase, '*Optimae Uxoris, Optimae Sororis, Viduus Amantissimus Vovit Virtutibus*', that is, 'Best wife, best sister, the most loving widower dedicates [this] to [your] virtue'.[23]

The Anson family and their interests place the monument firmly in the context of the eighteenth-century view of a classical elegiac Arcadia. Nothing connects it with the grail or the Templars. The tomb in the painting is imaginary. Only much later was a structure (possibly) built in the French countryside, and even later still was it linked to the tomb in the painting. Since the inscribed tomb did not exist when Poussin painted his vision of shepherds in Arcadia, a connection with the Anson family who commissioned the Shugborough monument in the eighteenth century is unlikely in the extreme.

The supposedly esoteric beliefs of the revived and restored Templars and Cathars add a mythic dimension to popular interpretations of history. They provide occult movements with links to the past, while at the same time they embody modern values. In the context of contemporary thinking, Templar and Cathar beliefs have been transformed into respect for nature and enlightened gender politics. As such they have been embraced by the tourist industry, by both liberal and right-wing political movements, by new age pilgrims and by modern conspiracy theory. Freed from the constraints of historical accuracy, these modern perspectives exploit the dramatic potential of what they perceive as an attempt to conceal eternal truth. The purpose of the myth is always the transmission of secret wisdom, although details may vary. When the legend took shape during the eighteenth century, older ideas about the unity of creation were combined with new esoteric speculations about secret societies to create an apparently unbroken line of transmission from ancient to modern civilization. Metaphors and parables about the past were woven together, and where evidence of connections was lacking, or at best tenuous, secrecy was used to bridge the gap. By the nineteenth-century, groups like the Templars and the Cathars had been rehabilitated as defenders of freedom and possessors of wisdom beneficial to humanity, and new organisations used them as models for further speculation.

Ideas about the origins of the grail transformed the grail quest in medieval romance into a metaphor for personal and cultural achievement. Theories about alternative grail quests abound, and it would be impossible to review all of them, much less the vast range of comment on the Internet and elsewhere. However, all these theories share two assumptions; first that the grail legend conceals a secret, and second that the guardians of the grail are targeted by a sinister conspiracy mounted by the establishment. The secret and the conspiracy add the thrill of a detective story to the adventures of the grail knights. As a result the audience participates in the adventures once assigned to medieval heroes and becomes personally involved in unscrambling the clues to discover a secret

'Perceval's Dream' from Morte d'Arthur, Robert Southey (ed.) (London: 1817).

Left: *Peredur in the Castle of Wonders from* The Mabinogion, *Charlotte Guest (tr.), 1877 edition.*

Below: *Castell Dinas Bran and its environs, by Joseph Pennell.*

Left: 'Perceval on Quest' from Sir Gawain at the Grail Castle, Jessie Weston.

Below: The West Front of Strata Florida Abbey.

WEST FRONT
STRATA FLORIDA ABBEY

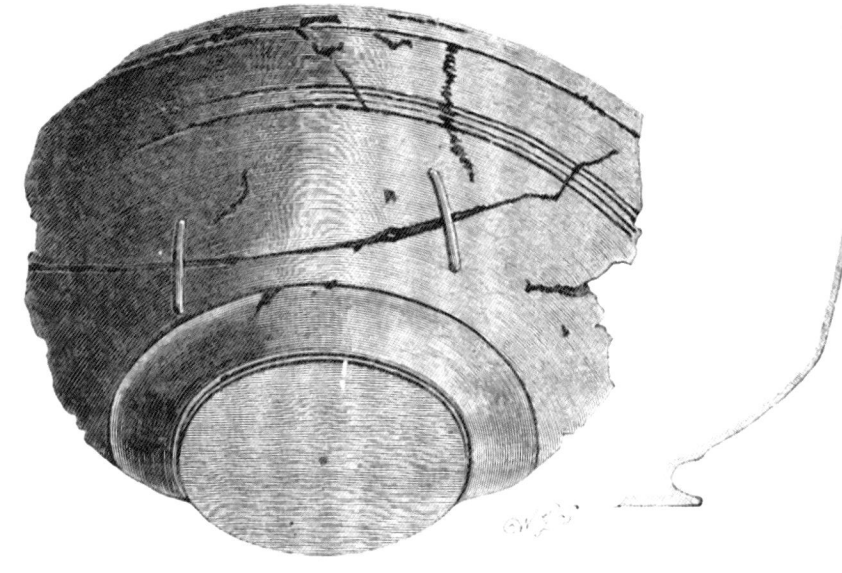

THE NANTEOS CUP.

Above: The Nanteos Cup, J. Worthington Smith, Archeologia Cambrensis.

Right: Welsh translations of the Prophecies of James Usher and others (1828?).

DAROGANAU
A
PHROPHWYDOLIAETH
HYNOD A RHYFEDDOL
Y duwiol a'r dysgedig

JAMES USHER,
Diw. Arch=esgob Armagh,
A
PHRIF-ESGOB Y WERDDON OLL;
YN CYNNWYS RHAG-FYNEGIAD

Am y Gwrthryfel yn y Werddon, ddeugain mlynedd cyn iddo gymeryd lle; y Terfysgoedd a'r Adfyd yn Mrydain mewn gwlad ac eglwys; marwolaeth y brenin Charles I.; ei Dylodi a'i Angen ef ei hun; yr Ymraniadau y'Mrydain mewn achosion crefyddol; gyda'r Erledigaeth fawr ac arswydus sydd i ddisgyn ar yr Eglwysi Diwygiedig drwy ddwylaw y Pabyddion.

AT YR HYN Y CHWANEGWYD

Prophwydoliaeth Ryfeddol
Y NODEDIG
ROBERT NIXON,
O Swydd Gaer Lleon;
YR HON SYDD YN RHAG-FYNEGI
AMRYW DDYGWYDDIADAU HYNOD
PERTHYNOL I FRYDAIN FAWR;
Y'NGHYD A
DESGRIFIAD BYR O'R PROPHWYD HWNW.

CAERNARFON,
ARGRAFFWYD AC AR WERTH GAN PETER EVANS.

Gwerth Chwe' Cheiniog.

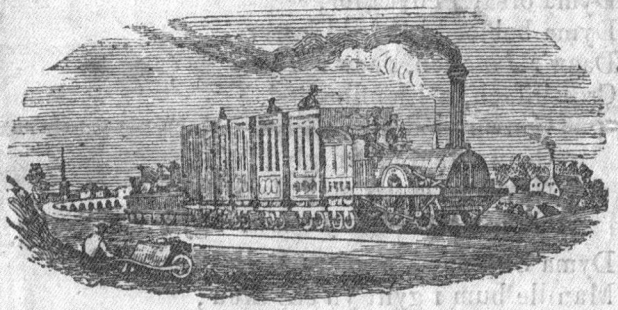

Manchester & Milford Railway.

CAN NEWYDD,

SEF

Taith gyda'r Railway

O

BENFRO I STRATA FLORIDA

Yng nghyd ag ychydig sylwadau ar y Gwaith
oddi yno i Aberystwyth.

Ar y Don Fechan,

Pwff, pwff mae'r Train yn starto,
Yn y boreu o Sir Benyfro ;
Dyma gyfle am Manchester
Neu unrhyw ran o Gymru a Lloeger,

Manchester & Milford Railway broadside ballad, 'Taith gyda'r Railway o Benfro
i Strata Florida' (n.d.).

CHAPELS, MONUMENTS AND RELICS

L ITERATURE AND ART from the Victorian period to the present incorporate themes and images relating to the grail[1] and renewed interest in the origin and meaning of these stories paralleled this literary and artistic revival. Scholars began to ask whether the grail was an authentic relic of the Passion of Christ brought back from the Holy Land during the Crusades or was it a religious relic associated with early British Christianity, and if so, where was it kept? These questions still resonate in contemporary grail traditions. They are reflected in legends that surround objects that claim to be the actual Holy Grail cup used at the Last Supper and in stories about the places where the grail might be hidden.

In Robert de Boron's romance of *Joseph of Arimathea*, the Holy Grail is one of the most important relics associated with the Passion of Jesus Christ. Many popular characterizations of the grail have tended to play down the Christian meaning in favour of possible pagan, esoteric or alternative Christian roots. However the Christian symbolism of the grail is a prominent feature in the medieval romances, and once the grail was identified with the Last Supper vessel, it was usually described as a chalice or a reliquary. Hermits and chapels were significant romance themes, and they added to the general atmosphere of Christian holiness. Perceval's reaction to his initial failure at the Fisher King's castle is to avoid entering a church, in effect cutting himself off from religion. Only after he meets his uncle the hermit and is reunited with his faith can he accomplish his task.

Chapels are important locations in the grail quest. An adventure undertaken by Perceval and Gawain takes place in a sinister chapel in which the body of a knight is laid out and a mysterious black hand appears and extinguishes the candles. This is one of the adventures that became known as the Perilous Chapel, and commentators like Jessie Weston endowed it with deep esoteric significance.[2] The adulterous Lancelot falls asleep outside a chapel containing the grail, while an injured knight is cured in its presence. Perhaps the most dramatic chapel scene concerns the grail mass in which Joseph of Arimathea's son, Josephus, celebrates mass with the grail cup, and the knights witness the grail transformed into a series of Eucharistic images. However, when Lancelot touches the grail in an attempt to help a frail priest who is serving mass, he falls back as if struck, and an angelic hand reaches out to catch the sacred vessel.

Although several knights actually achieve the quest of the Holy Grail in the medieval romances, the grail itself apparently vanishes at the end of the quest. This of course opened the way for speculation about its 'true' meaning and origin and in particular about where it might be hidden.

ROSSLYN CHAPEL

Rosslyn Chapel is one of the locations put forward as a possible hiding place for the Holy Grail. The chapel is located near the village of Roslin in Midlothian, Scotland, and, at first glance, it looks like a miniature version of a medieval cathedral. It is covered inside and out with intricate carving and architectural ornament. One of the first mystical re-interpretations of the site compared its architecture to that of the Perilous Chapel of the grail romances,[3] but more recently traditions about Templars have dominated the folklore associated with Rosslyn.

William St Clair, Third Earl of Orkney and First Earl of Caithness (1402–86) began construction of the Collegiate Church of St Matthew in 1446. A collegiate church was serviced by canons – priests who lived within the precinct and followed a religious life, but were not monks. One of their duties was to pray for the patrons of the church, in this case the St Clair family, and to ensure that they were given decent

Christian burial. The church at Rosslyn was never completed, and what remains today, known as Rosslyn Chapel, is the oblong choir, a Lady Chapel dedicated to the Virgin Mary and a small room beneath this chapel. Many collegiate churches became parish churches after the Reformation, and some like Rosslyn, which was off the beaten track, continued in limited use under the control of Protestant clergy.

The original building dates from the fifteenth century, and its most striking feature is the wealth of carving on every available surface. These carvings are the focus for numerous ingenious speculations about William St Clair's alleged involvement with the Holy Grail. Not all the decoration is contemporary with the original building, as work continued after the earl's death and periodic restorations have been carried out. A significant portion of this restoration coincides with a rise of Freemasonry during the eighteenth century when the much-damaged chapel was repaired and reopened. Traditions associating it with the grail are even more recent. It was singled out as a 'Conspiracy site' in *The Holy Blood and the Holy Grail* and has now become firmly established as a secret grail venue thanks to a series of books published in the 1990s which fused well-established alternative history themes about Freemasons and Templars into a Scottish version of the grail legend.[4]

Briefly, the secret history of Rosslyn suggests that some knights escaped before the arrest of the Templars in France in 1307. They fled in Templar ships with a secret talisman from the site of Solomon's Temple in Jerusalem and sought shelter with Robert the Bruce. The timely intervention of these escaping Templars allegedly ensured Scottish victory at the Battle of Bannochburn (1314). The grateful Scottish monarch created the Order of Freemasons as a cover for the fugitive Templar knights, and a century later, the Sinclair family, secret Grand Masters of the Templars, built Rosslyn Chapel to house this powerful talisman. The imagery in the Chapel allegedly provides a key to this secret history and to the hiding place of the treasure. Based on this alternative view of history, carvings in Rosslyn have been identified with historical figures, like Robert the Bruce, and Masonic heroes, like Hiram, the master builder of Solomon's temple and countless 'grail' shapes have been identified. Attempts have been made to find a 'key' to a supposedly secret meaning behind the carvings, and documents have been used as 'coded maps' to locate the hiding place of the Holy Grail.[5]

The Rosslyn Chapel carvings have been repaired and altered over time. One of the main legends associated with the chapel is that of a gifted apprentice who carved the large and ornate Apprentice Pillar that dominates the chapel and was killed by the jealous master mason. A carving supposed to represent this apprentice is one of the decorations that may have been altered later with the addition of wound-like gashes to enhance the legend of the murdered apprentice. Other carvings interpreted as Masonic or Templar images feature regularly in esoteric interpretations of Rosslyn, although most actually fit into an orthodox schema of Christian iconography that illustrates the fall and redemption of humankind. Such 'bibles in stone', as they have been called, were not unusual. Although there was no universal or consistent system for depicting or interpreting religious symbolism, the ambiguities do not point to esoteric secrets. Rosslyn's oddity lies in the fact that it remained largely intact, despite Reformation reaction against distracting and idolatrous iconography, and the chapel stands out more today than it would have done when it was built.

The idea that the grail is hidden in the chapel is a comparatively recent layer of myth based on several well-known legends that are localized at Rosslyn Chapel. Although the legends reflect ongoing interest in this fascinating site, they cannot be patched together to form a convincing history. The belief that Oliver Cromwell's soldiers stabled horses in religious buildings is one of these traditions. As there was no wholesale destruction of the chapel at Rosslyn, it has been suggested that Cromwell himself might have been a Mason who hesitated to destroy an important site. As a popular folk villain, Cromwell is a rather wayward figure destroying or sparing life and property at a whim. Another tradition is attached to the intricately carved Apprentice Pillar, which is certainly one of Rosslyn's most striking features. One account specifically says that the 'apprentice' story is a legend and notes that the carved head pointed out as that of the murdered apprentice has been altered to conform to the details of the tale. Earlier sources call the strikingly carved column in the chapel the 'Prince's pillar, and this implies that the story about the jealous master mason killing his apprentice was added later. The murder of

Solomon's master mason, Hiram, an important legend for Freemasons and Masonic lore may have contributed to a reinterpretation of the Rosslyn carvings. The addition of the apprentice legend at the end of the eighteenth century may reflect the popularity of traditions about Hiram rather than the memory of an ancient sect. In any case, the apprentice story is not unique to Rosslyn, and the theme of the envious artisan murdering a competitor is attached to other trades.[6]

Nothing has been found at Rosslyn despite several 'archaeological' investigations, but hopes have not been entirely dashed by those who think the grail is there. When excavations were undertaken in the 1990s soon after the publication of books about the Scottish grail, a crude cup was uncovered in the vault beneath the chapel. This was probably left by an earlier workman and no one suggested seriously that it was the grail, but one of the charms of these grail legends is the way in which the possibility of a dramatic discovery overshadows mundane reality.

GRAIL RELICS

The night before the Crucifixion, Jesus and the apostles observed the Jewish feast of Passover. This event is known as the Last Supper. At this time, Christ blessed bread and wine saying that it was his body and blood, and this became the sacrament of the Eucharist.[7] Robert de Boron identified the Holy Grail of the romances with the cup used to hold the wine at that last Passover feast. Despite the popularity of the grail theme in romance, medieval traditions about the Last Supper cup are rare in comparison with other legends associated with Christ's final days like the True Cross or the Spear of Longinus. The history of the grail in the post-romance period is rich and varied and it has become more prominent in contemporary legends. Both Dr Goodchild and Lionel Smithett Lewis drew parallels between the grail at Glastonbury and the Last Supper, although one focused on an antique Italian glass curio, the other on a wooden cup. Both objects have contributed to the mystical reputations of Glastonbury and Wales, but other objects are also associated with the Last Supper, and the mysterious chapels in the romances lead to other places where the Holy Grail might be hidden. Valencia Cathedral possesses a semi-precious stone bowl set in silver gilt and used as a chalice. A damaged green glass dish is displayed in the museum attached to Genoa's cathedral, and a late-classical silver-gilt liturgical object is now in a New York Museum. All these objects have their own 'histories' steeped in local tradition and often mixed with Templar legends and mass-market conspiracy theories.

Early references suggest that Eucharistic vessels were originally ordinary glass or pottery containers, and late classical mosaics and sarcophagi depict double-handled objects with short broad bases. Chalices of wood and other materials were used for private services, but these were eventually considered inappropriate for such a sacred event. By the time the romances were written, specially crafted vessels in precious metal were used, and these developed a characteristic shape consisting of a cup with a short stem, often with a round knob to make it easier to hold, and a broad base for stability.

Initially Eucharist services were celebrated in private homes, but as the structure of the ritual began to crystallize with the spread of Christianity, private services were transferred to purpose-built churches. By the thirteenth century, the Church had begun to encourage lay Christians, namely those who were not in religious orders, to participate in the sacrament of communion on a regular basis. At the same time theological debate over the meaning of the doctrine and ritual was taking place and new Eucharistic devotions were becoming popular. These included the 'elevation' of the host and chalice during the mass and a special feast-day, the Feast of Corpus Christi (Latin for 'the body of Christ'). Artistic representations of the Eucharist depicted the risen Christ appearing from the Mass chalice, and distinctive rituals at which the priest blessed the congregation with the consecrated host or displayed it on the altar in an elaborate container were introduced and became popular. New themes appeared in the grail romances, for example Joseph of Arimathea's role, as well as more abstract spiritual ideas about how the grail nourished and comforted the faithful. The grail feast celebrated by Joseph of Arimathea and his followers in Robert de Boron's romance provided a link between the institution of the Eucharist at the Last Supper and the Round Table of Arthur's court. Similar symbolic links between the grail and the Eucharist appear in other romances. Gawain has a striking vision in which he sees a transformed grail in the form of the child Jesus and then as the risen Christ, while Arthur and Perceval witness an almost mystical grail mass in *Perlesvaus*. However, it is worth stressing that the romances were not works of pious devotion and these incidents, although detailed and poetic, always fall within the bounds of orthodox Christian thinking.[8]

The New Testament of the Christian Bible tells the story of the life of Jesus Christ and the early ministry of the Apostles. The events surrounding Christ's death are collectively referred to as the Passion. Even after the canonical accounts of Christ's life were established in the New Testament, a number of non-canonical (or apocryphal) texts remained part of Christian devotion. Some were widely read and translated, others fell out of use or exist in fragments and some were lost. Robert de Boron's romance was the first to incorporate legends about St Joseph of Arimathea from non-canonical apocryphal works. On the occasion of the Last Supper, which coincided with the Jewish festival of Passover, Christ blessed bread and wine, an action commemorated in the Christian mass as the Eucharist. In the romances the cup used at this meal became identified with the grail. Other events also found their way into the grail romances and into modern grail legends as well. Christ's mother, the Virgin Mary, St John the Evangelist and Mary Magdalene witnessed the Crucifixion, which ended when a Roman solder, later identified as the centurion Longinus, pierced Christ's side with a lance. The body was removed from the cross and a man named Joseph of Arimathea offered to bury the body in his own tomb. Later traditions say that Joseph collected the blood from Christ's wounds in the same cup used at the Last Supper, which had been given to him by the Roman governor, Pontius Pilate.

Perhaps the earliest reference to a relic of the Last Supper occurs in the account of an Irish pilgrim named Arculf who visited the Holy Land sometime in the seventh century. Among the many wonders he recorded during this journey was an account of a two-handled silver chalice in a chapel near Golgotha, the site of the crucifixion. The object is not called a grail, and even at this early period there is some confusion about its appearance. Arculf's description refers to a silver relic, but another account claims it was made of onyx.[9] Nearly a thousand years later, the Protestant Archbishop James Ussher linked the grail to the story of St Joseph of Arimathea at Glastonbury Abbey, although no object was identified as the Holy Grail in Glastonbury until the beginning of the twentieth century. Besides Ussher's account, there are two other seventeenth-century references to the cup used at the Last Supper, one at an abbey near Lyon in France, another at Troyes. Neither of these is called the Holy Grail, but the origin and ultimate fate of the chalice at Troyes reflects some features of other grail legends. According to tradition, it was looted from a church in the Holy Land during the Crusades and disappeared during the French Revolution. As with so many contemporary legend motifs, it is at least credible as there is no supernatural agency involved and the events take place in an uncontested historical time frame. However, such traditions are also a regular feature of origin legends about sacred objects, not just the grail, and while the French Revolution, the Reformation, the English Civil War and the Napoleonic period were times of social upheaval, they provide a context for mysterious disappearances and dramatic rescues in a whole range of legends.

The veneration of relics was important in popular devotion during the middle ages. In the wake of the Crusades, numerous accounts circulated about miraculous discoveries, daring escapes and ingenious methods of transporting precious objects from enemy hands to western churches. Several 'grail' relics have legendary contacts with the Crusades. The 'emerald' vessel of Genoa, the *sacro catino*, was 'discovered' in a mosque in Caesarea and brought to Europe. The historian of the Crusades, William of Tyre, whose *History of Deeds Beyond the Sea* is also a source for legends about the Templars, claimed it was carved from a single emerald. It was brought to Genoa by a crusader, Guglielmo Embriaco, the founder of an influential Genoese family. However, an alternative tradition claims that the *sacro catino* was given to Genoese mercenaries by the Spanish king in recognition for their aid in the wars against the Moors. The *sacro catino* is in fact a shallow hexagonal glass dish, about eighteen inches across. The rim has been damaged, allegedly when Napoleon looted the object. Before it was returned to Genoa, it was found to be green glass, not precious emerald. Napoleon, like Henry VIII and Oliver Cromwell, functions as a generic villain in legends such as these. They all attempt to discredit or steal some precious object, but always fail.

Early sources did not identify the *sacro catino* with the grail, and it seems to have been a valuable rather than a sacred object. However emerald was not just a precious gem, it had magical and medical properties as well. When the bishop of Genoa, Jacobus of Voragine, wrote about the city's glorious past at the end of the thirteenth century, the object became part of Genoese crusade history and was identified with the Last Supper. Jacobus described the *sacro catino* as the emerald dish from which Christ and his apostles ate the Pascal lamb at that final Passover supper and cited 'English books' which speak of the Sangraal, thus linking the object with the grail romances. A fresco in the Palazzo San Giorgio in Genoa shows Guglielmo Embriaco holding the *sacro catino*, and it is now housed in a museum attached to San Lorenzo Cathedral. It is still an important part of Genoese heritage, and a copy is paraded through the streets during public festivals.[10]

The varied accounts of the *sacro catino*, and other grail relics, encapsulate how legend can confer meaning and significance on ordinary objects and transform them into relics. The typical form of such a legend begins with a mysterious history; often this is set in the context of the Crusades with odd and inexplicable details that suggest the object dates from the beginning of Christian history. The object is lost for a time, often because of the machinations of some famous villain. However, someone – a local hero or saint – hides and protects the object and finally there is a dramatic restoration.

Traditions like these about mysterious heritage and miraculous discovery surround the *santo caliz* in Valencia Cathedral in Spain. This 'grail' is a small agate bowl set in a gilt-framed mounting, so it can be used as a chalice for celebrating mass. The *santo caliz* could be a Greco-Roman artefact although stone artefacts like this are difficult to date and such chalices are not unusual. Unfortunately, actual historical records, as opposed to traditions, associated with it are not particularly early. It may have been in the possession of the king of Aragon in the fourteenth century, but there is no solid information about its earlier history. Not surprisingly, an alternative, unverifiable, imaginative history surrounds the *santo caliz* and mirrors legends attached to other grail objects. According to the Spanish legend, St Peter and St Lawrence, rather than Joseph of Arimathea, are the guardians of the *santo caliz*. St Peter took the cup with him to Rome and gave it to St Lawrence for safekeeping, and an unnamed guardian hid the cup in a monastery during the Moorish invasions. King Alfonso V of Aragon sold the cup to the cathedral of Valencia in the fifteenth century. This may possibly reflect Spanish royal interest in chivalry and in the grail romances, and later Spanish paintings of the Last Supper seem to depict this object or one very like it. The *santo caliz* is now housed in an elaborate chapel in Valencia Cathedral. It remains an important icon in its local setting, but veneration is based on its symbolic links to the Eucharist story rather than the grail romances.[11]

Several new grails became prominent at the beginning of the twentieth century. Among them was the damaged medieval wooden bowl known as the Nanteos cup, and an antique glass dish that came to light just outside Glastonbury, England.[12] In the 1930s, two archaeological finds appeared briefly as candidates for the grail. One, a drinking cup fitted with a protective leather case, was exhibited in London among other Biblical artefacts. According to a somewhat vague tradition, a crusader brought it back from the East. The other, more famous example, is a magnificent silver-gilt object originally identified as a Eucharist cup, and probably crafted at Antioch during the sixth century. Gustavus Eisen, a colourful but respected antiquary, dated it to the beginning of the Christian era and suggested that the elaborate outer shell protected a plain inner cup which he identified with the Holy Grail. It was displayed with great fanfare at the Chicago World's Fair of 1933–4 and is now in the Metropolitan Museum of Art in New York. The exquisite silver adornment depicts men sitting among a running motif of vine and grapes. The figures have been identified as the apostles or as classical philosophers whose work was thought to prefigure Christianity. The object is probably a liturgical lamp rather than a chalice, which would suggest that the decoration relates to Christ as the light of the world, not the Last Supper. Nevertheless, the Antioch Chalice featured in a successful sword-and-sandals historical novel and film of the 1950s, *The Silver Chalice*. The plot revolved around the adventures of a young pagan silversmith who was commissioned by Joseph of Arimathea to provide a container for the cup used at the Last Supper. The young man sought out the followers of Christ in order to sculpt their likenesses. Naturally, he found both adventure and romance with a beautiful Christian girl and converted to the new faith.[13] The Antioch chalice has had something of an afterlife in film as the basis for the comical Holy Hand Grenade of Antioch sought by the knights of *Monty Python and the Holy Grail*.[14]

The account of these grail relics follows a distinctive pattern. Their history is always shrouded in mystery, but a line of custodians, linked by mysterious coincidences, leads back through some early Christian figure to the events surrounding the Last Supper. The line of custodians, and these often include Templars and crusaders, provide a narrative thread for other elements of the legend, since concrete sources are always missing. The chaos of the Crusades or the confusion surrounding the trial of the Templars fills the vacuum left by imperfect documentation. The story of the *santo caliz* leads back to St Peter through Spanish kings and saints, and the *sacro catino* was brought to Genoa by a crusader. Invariably, the grail comes into the possession of its present owner in dramatic or mysterious circumstances. The last survivor among the guardian monks supposedly gave the Nanteos Cup to the Powell family, while the owner of the Glastonbury grail concealed his glass bowl so that it could be found in the most dramatic way possible.

When the English theologian Robert Grosseteste wrote about Westminster Abbey's acquisition of a relic of the Holy Blood, he drew on the apocryphal *Gospel of Nicodemus* for the story of Joseph of Arimathea. The theological description is more concerned with the sacred blood than with the container, but Grosseteste refers to Joseph gathering and preserving the blood still flowing from the wounds of the dead Christ as he was being prepared for burial. Westminster was one of several medieval pilgrimage sites that possessed a relic of the Holy Blood. Others include Fécamp Abbey in France, Bruges in Belgium and Hailes Abbey in Gloucestershire. The relics at Hailes and Westminster were gifts from the Patriarch of Jerusalem during a period of relatively successful Crusade activity in the second half of the thirteenth century. Both English relics were destroyed during the Reformation, but it is possible that the relic at Hailes Abbey influenced Thomas Malory's description of the Holy Grail. Malory lived near the Abbey and would have seen the relic. John Hardyng, a near contemporary of Malory, also adapted the grail romances, and he interpreted the term 'Sank Royal' as 'royal blood'.[15] Medieval grail romances were not devotional literature, but neither did they advocate unorthodox ideas. For both writers, the characterisation of the relic was consistent with a lay understanding of Eucharistic doctrine and practice prior to the Reformation. In contrast, many modern narratives associated with grail relics follow a pattern in which code, revelation and secret message are dominant themes, and the idea of *sang real* took a dramatic turn in the 1980s with the publication of that ingeniously speculative and popular example of the conspiracy genre, *The Holy Blood and The Holy Grail*.

The search for a real grail reflects a need for the supernatural in a sceptical and secular age. Unlike earlier relics, which were a source of miraculous cures, current grail relics are not primarily a source for miracles. Cures are attached to the Nanteos cup, but they are not a feature of other modern grail legends. Scientific disciplines like archaeology and carbon dating rather than miracles are often the means used to authenticate contemporary grail relics. The Great Chalice of Antioch and the Glastonbury glass bowl were viewed initially as archaeological antiquities and expert opinion was sought to examine them. A few popular studies have even attempted to reaffirm the archaeological authenticity of the Genoese *sacro catino*. Science was a means by which the irrational world was brought under secular control discrediting many relics in the process. However the use of science has become part of the legendary frame of modern grail legends. If the power of these relics has been neutralized by the rise of science and reason, alternative theories attempt to resanctify such relics by using the same techniques that demystified them. A tension between the grail as archaeological artefact and sacred object is a feature of several modern grails.[16] Archaeology plays an important role as a way to investigate the physical traces of the past and provide a means for accessing and displaying that past.

As a result the grail as an archaeological object but with hidden powers is a prominent theme in modern grail fiction and film. Films such as *Lancelot du Lac* (1974), *Perceval le Gallois* (1978) and *Excalibur*

(1981)[17] treat the grail quest in the context of an Arthurian world, but other films use an archaeological discovery as a device to bring the grail into the modern world. In an early silent film *The Light in the Dark* (1922),[18] a grail which glows in the dark is discovered in the ruins of an English abbey and displayed at the home of a wealthy New York businessman. Lon Chaney steals it in an attempt to cure a sick young woman and its power eventually reunites two lovers. The screenwriter, and author of the story on which the film was based, William Dudley Pelley, was a political activist with extreme views and an interest in spiritualism. The film leaves unresolved the question as to whether this is the 'true' Holy Grail or whether its unearthly glow is the result of a radioactive substance placed there by a conman.

The pivotal event in many modern grail treatments hangs on a character's ability to recognise the true nature of an object seemingly found by chance, like the one found in a well in Mary Butts's novel, *Armed with Madness*, or in a churchyard in Charles Williams's *War in Heaven*.[19] In Susan Cooper's *The Dark is Rising*, a chalice discovered by a group of children in a sea cave in Cornwall is both a relic of Celtic paganism and a physical archaeological antiquity.[20] Indiana Jones has to choose the least prepossessing object from an array of chalices in order to identify the true grail and save his father. His choice is the most convincing as an archaeological artefact and as the cup of a simple fisherman, in other words the real grail. In Bernard Cornwell's grail trilogy, the grail seekers find a mysterious empty box in the Languedoc and realize that the true grail, an ordinary clay vessel, has been in the hero's home village all the time. Cornwell's is a very modern treatment of the legend. Like the hero, Indiana Jones, the grail seeker's defining characteristic is not to ask a question, but to be able to distinguish between real and false grails.

It is just possible that the description of a two-handled silver chalice seen by Arculf the pilgrim may have influenced the shape and decoration of the famous Ardagh Chalice from Ireland. This imposing object was found together with a much simpler bronze mass chalice, buried in a ditch in Ardagh, County Limerick, Ireland in 1868 by the son of a widowed farmer who was digging under a thorn tree. The story of its discovery is typical of traditions about archaeological finds, and like so many legends of this type, it could be true. The story of a humble boy finding a treasure almost by accident confers further distinction on a famous object. The chalice found at Ardagh has never been linked to the grail of romance or to a relic from the Last Supper, but the possibility that Arculf's description may have influenced the appearance of later vessels, if true, would bring this brief history of grail relics to a very neat conclusion

CONCLUSION

MUCH HAS CHANGED our understanding of the grail since Chrétien introduced it into his romance in the twelfth century. Robert de Boron identified it as the cup used by Christ at the Last Supper and transformed it into the Holy Grail. In its literary form, the medieval grail reached a peak with Malory's *Le Morte Darthur*, but as a legend it has continued to develop. The links between the grail legend and the Joseph of Arimathea story, and the fusion of traditions about Arthur, St Joseph of Arimathea and Glastonbury, which began in the twelfth century, continues to the present day.

Today the Holy Grail is many things. It can be any desired objective, or the perfect solution to a problem or a secret just out of reach. By contrast the grail quest in medieval romance was always accomplished. The grail might elude an unworthy seeker, but the destined knight always found it.

Over time the grail legend has become independent of its origins in many ways. Sometimes the object is a physical relic, sometimes it is knowledge expressed in words or actions, sometimes it is a mystic experience. While grail fictions written in the past century have realigned some of the polarities found in medieval sources for the grail narrative, both medieval and modern versions narrate the actions of a character on a life-changing journey. The debate about the origin and meaning of the grail reflects changing cultural fashions. Whether the grail was believed to be a sacred myth, an initiation rite, an archetype or set of beliefs among Celts or Christians, or the contemporary fashion for secret codes, the search for the grail was often the search for its ultimate origin.

The relationship between grail and the grail seeker has also changed. Modern interpretations may favour conspiracies and secret codes, but they are linked to medieval grail romances by the idea of quest. The grail seeker must be able to distinguish between real and false grails, rather than ask the question which opens the way to a vision of the Holy Grail, but it is a quest all the same. However it changes, the grail still has the power to inspire readers and to send them on their own imaginative journey.

NOTES

1 THE SOURCES OF THE GRAIL ROMANCES

1   Juliette Wood, *Eternal Chalice; the Enduring Legend of the Holy Grail* (London: I. B. Tauris, 2008), 9–28, Richard Barber, *The Holy Grail Imagination and Belief* (London: Alan Lane, 2004), 9–86.

2   Chrétien de Troyes, *Perceval the Story of the Grail*, Nigel Bryant (tr.) (Cambridge and Totowa NJ: Brewer, 1982).

3   *The Continuations of the Old French Perceval of Chrétien de Troyes* William Roach (ed.) (Philadelphia: University of Pennsylvania Press, 1949–1983).

4   *Bliocadran: A Prologue to the Perceval of Chrétien de Troyes*, Leonora Wolfgang (ed.) (Tubingen: Niemeyer, 1976).

5   *The Elucidation: A Prologue to the Conte del Graal*, Albert Wilder Thompson (ed.) (1931) (Genève: Slatkine, 1982).

6   Robert de Boron, *L'estoire del Saint Graal*, Jean-Paul Ponceau (ed.), Classiques Français du Moyen Age (Paris, 1997); *Merlin and the Grail: Joseph of Arimathea, Merlin and Perceval: the trilogy of prose romances attributed to Robert de Boron*, Nigel Bryant (tr.), *Arthurian studies* 48 (Cambridge and Rochester, New York, 2001); Robert de Boron, *Le Roman du graal: Manuscrit de Modène*, Bernard Cerquigliani (ed. and tr.) (Paris, 1981).

7   Robert de Boron, *Le Roman de L'Estoire dou Graal*, William A. Nitze (ed.) (Paris, 1927; repr. 1983).

8   *The Didot Perceval*, William Roach (ed.) (Philadelphia: University of Pennsylvania Press), 1971), D. Skeeles (tr.) (Seattle: University of Washington Press, 1966.)

9   *Perlesvaus or The High Book of the Grail*, Nigel Bryant (tr.) (Cambridge: University Press, 1978), *Perceval le Gallois, Perlesvaus. The High Book of the Grail:*

a translation of the thirteenth century romance of 'Perlesvaus' translated and introduced by Nigel Bryant (Cambridge & Totowa, 1978).

10 Y *Seint Greal*, Robert Williams (ed.) (London: T. Richards, 1876).

11 'Peredur son of Efrog', 65–102 in *The Mabinogion*, Sioned Davies (tr.) (Oxford University Press, 2007).

12 Wolfram von Eschenbach, *Parzival*, A. T. Hatto (tr.) (London: Penguin, 1980).

13 *Lancelot-Grail: The Old French Arthurian Vulgate and Post-Vulgate in Translation*, Norris J. Lacy (ed.) (New York, 1993–6), *The Vulgate Version of the Arthurian Romance*, H. O. Sommer (ed.), 8 vols (repr. New York: The Carnegie Institution, 1979); *The Grail Quest*, P. M. Matarasso (ed. and tr.) (Harmondsworth: Penguin, 1969).

14 Heinrich von der Türlin, *The Crown* (Diu Crône) J. W. Thomas (tr.) (Lincoln and London: University of Nebraska Press, 1989).

15 *Fouke le Fitz Waryn*, E. J. Hathaway et al. (eds), Anglo-Norman Text Society (Oxford: Blackwell, 1975).

16 *Sone de Nansay et le roman d'aventures en vers au 13e siècle*, Claude Lachet (ed.) (Genèva: Slatkine, 1992).

17 *Le Roman de Tristan en prose*, Gilles Roussineau (ed.) (Geneva: Librairie Droz, 1991).

18 *The Works of Sir Thomas Malory*, Eugene Vinaver (ed.) (Oxford: Oxford University Press, 1954; P. J. C. Field (rev.) 1990) Book 1, Book 5, Book 6 lines 845–6.

19 Barber, 215–21; *A Companion to Malory*, Elizabeth Archibald and A. S. G. Edwards (eds) (Cambridge: D. S. Brewer, 1996), 115–30.

20 Wood, 36–7; Barber, 215, 227–8.

3 VISIONS OF THE GRAIL

1 'The Tale of Peredur son of Efrog' 65–102 in *The Mabinogion*, Sioned Davies (tr.) (Oxford University Press, 2007).

2 Juliette Wood, 'A Welsh Triad: Charlotte Guest, Marie Trevelyan, Mary Williams', 259–76, in *Women and Tradition: A Neglected Group of Folklorists*, Carmen Blacker and Hilda Davidson (eds) (Durham, North Carolina: Carolina Academic Press, 2000).

3 Robert Southey, *The birth lyf and actes of kyng Arthur* [Morte d'Arthur] (London, 1817).

4 Alfred Lord Tennyson, *The Holy Grail and Other Poems* (London: Strahan and Co., 1870), *The Idylls of the King* (Boston: Ticknor and Fields, 1859).

5   James Russell Lowell, *The Vision of Sir Launfal* (8th edn) (Boston: Ticknor and Fields, 1863).

6   'Branwen', 22–34, 'Manawydan', 'Culhwch ac Olwen', 179–213, 'Lludd a Llefellys', 111–15, 'Iarlles y Ffynwn', 116–38 in *The Mabinogion*, Davies (tr.).

7   Roger Sherman Loomis, *The Grail: from Celtic Myth to Christian Symbol* (Cardiff: University of Wales Press, 1963); John Carey, *Ireland and the Grail* (Aberystwyth: Celtic Studies Publications, 2007).

8   Alfred Nutt, *Studies in the Legend of the Holy Grail: with especial reference to the hypothesis of its Celtic origin* (London: David Nutt, 1888).

9   Jessie L. Weston, *From Ritual to Romance*, 1925 repr. (Princeton: Princeton University Press, 1993).

10   Juliette Wood, 'The Holy Grail: From Romance Motif to Modern Genre', *Folklore* 111 (2000), 169–90.

11   T. S. Eliot, *Collected Poems* 1909–1962 (London: Faber and Faber, 1963), 'The Waste Land', 61–79, Notes 80–1; C. B. Cox and Arnold P. Hinchliffe (eds), T. S. *Eliot, The Waste Land: A Casebook* (London: Macmillan, 1968).

12   A. E. Waite, *The Holy Grail: Its Legends and Symbolism* (London: Rider, 1933), *The Hidden Church of the Holy Grail* (London: Rider, 1909).

13   Tom Gibbons, 'The Wasteland Tarot Identified', *Journal of Modern Literature* 2 (1972), 560–64.

14   Mary Butts, *Armed with Madness* (London: Wishart & Co., 1928).

15   John B. Marino, *The Grail Legend in Modern Literature*, Arthurian Studies LIX (Cambridge: Boydell & Brewer, 2004), 134–6.

16   Naomi Mitchison, *To the Chapel Perilous* (London: Allen, 1955).

17   A. A. Attanasio, *Kingdom of the Grail* (New York: Harper, 1992).

18   Dorothy James Roberts, *Kinsmen of the Grail* (Boston, Little, 1963).

19   David Jones, *The Anathemata* (London: Faber 1952, repr. 1955), *In Parenthesis* (London: Faber 1937), *The Sleeping Lord and other Fragments* (London: Faber 1974).

20   Jones, *The Sleeping Lord*, 74, 96.

21   Jones, *The Anathemata*, XVII, 20.

22   Wood, *Eternal Chalice*, 81–2, 169–71.

23   David Blamires, *David Jones: Artist and Writer* (2nd edn; Manchester: Manchester University Press, 1978), 180–2.

24   John Dyfnallt Owen, *Y Greal a Cherddi Eraill* (Gwasg Aberystwyth, 1946).

25   Edward Tegla Davies, *Y Greal Sanctaidd* (Wrecsam: Hughes, 1922).

26   Arthur Machen, *The Secret Glory* (East Sussex: Tartarus Press, 1998), chaps. V and VI.

27   Machen, *The Secret Glory*, 252; Wesley D. Sweetser, *Arthur Machen* (New York: Twayne, 1964), 32–4.

28   Arthur Machen, *The Secret of the Sangraal: A Collection of Writings* (East Sussex: Tartarus Press, 1994), 'The Secret of the Sangraal', 1–39, 'Celtic Magic', 142–5, 'The Holy Graal', 146–50, 'The Holy Grail', 228–32; Mark Valentine, *Arthur Machen* (Bridgend: Wales Poetry Press, 1995); Sweetser, *Arthur Machen* (New York: Twayne, 1964), 37–8.

29   Arthur Machen, 'The Great Return' in *Holy Terrors: Collected Short Stories* (London: Penguin, 1946), 108–40.

30   Wood, *Eternal Chalice* 68–9, 78–83.

31   Machen, 'The Holy Things' in *Holy Terrors*, 75–8; Machen, *Things Near and Far* (London: Richards Press, 1951).

32   Arthur Machen, 'Celtic Magic', 142–5.

33   John Carey, *Ireland and the Grail* (Aberystwyth: Celtic Studies Publications, 2007), 121–32.

34   Robert Graves, *The White Goddess: a Historical Grammar of Poetic Myth* (1948) new edn by Grevel Lindop (London: Faber and Faber, 1999).

35   Marion Zimmer Bradley, *The Mists of Avalon* (New York: Knopf, 1982).

36   Rosalind Miles, *Guenevere, The Child of the Holy Grail* (New York: Simon & Schuster, 2000).

37   *Excalibur*, John Boorman (dir.), 1981.

38   Susan Haskins, *Mary Magdalen: Myth and Metaphor* (London: Harper Collins, 1993).

39   Bernard Cornwell, *The Warlord Chronicles, The Winter King, Enemy of God, Excalibur* (London: Penguin, 1995–8); *The Grail Quest, Harlequin, Vagabond, Heretic* (London: HarperCollins, 2000–3).

40   Kate Mosse, *Labyrinth* (London: Orion, 2005).

41   Lawrence Schick, *Heroic Worlds: A History and Guide to Role-playing Games* (New York: Prometheus Press, 1991), 76–80.

42   Marcus L. Rowland, *Queen Victoria and the Holy Grail* (Games Workshop Ltd., 1985).

43   Jane Jensen, *Gabriel Knight 3: Blood of the Sacred, Blood of the Damned* (Sierra On-Line Games 1996).

44   Juliette Wood, 'The Creation of the Celtic Tarot', *Folklore* 109 (1998), 15–24.

4   FROM WALES TO GLASTONBURY

1   *The Early History of Glastonbury*: an edition, translation and study of William of Malmesbury's *De antiquitate Glastonie Ecclesie*, John Scott (ed.) (Woodbridge: Boydell & Brewer, 1981); James P. Carley (ed.), *Glastonbury Abbey and Arthurian Tradition* (Cambridge: D. S. Brewer, 2001), 30–9.

2   *The Chronicle of Glastonbury Abbey: an edition, translation and study of John of Glastonbury's 'Cronica sive antiquitates Glastoniensis ecclesie'*, James P. Carley (ed.), David Townsend (tr.) (Woodbridge, 1985); J. Armitage Robinson, *Two Glastonbury Legends: King Arthur and St. Joseph of Arimathea* (Cambridge, 1926); R. F. Treharne, *The Glastonbury Legends: Joseph of Arimathea, the Holy Grail and King Arthur* (London, 1967).

3   J. Wood, *Eternal Chalice*, 29–52; Barber, *The Holy Grail*, 131–4.

4   Carley, *Glastonbury Abbey*, 251–5, 269–84; Barber, 227–8.

5   Patrick Benham, *The Avalonians* (Glastonbury: Gothic Image Press 1993, rev. 2006); John Arthur Goodchild, *The Light of the West: An Account of the Dannite Settlement in Ireland* (London, 1898).

6   Dan Brown, *The Da Vinci Code* (New York: Bantam, 2003); Kate Mosse, *Labyrinth* (London: Orion, 2005).

7   Fiona MacLeod, *The Winged Destiny: the Spiritual History of the Gael* (London, 1904).

8   Juliette Wood, 'Obscure Objects of Desire: Is this the Real Holy Grail?' *www.juliettewood.com*.

9   Wood, *Eternal Chalice*, 38–43.

10   Marion Bowman, 'Procession and Possession in Glastonbury: Continuity, Change and Manipulation of Tradition', *Folklore* 115 (2004), 273–85; Ivakhiv, Adrian J., *Claiming Sacred Ground: Pilgrims and Politics at Glastonbury and Sedona* (Bloomington & Indianapolis, 2001).

11   Tracy Cutting, *Beneath the Silent Tor, the Life and Work of Alice Buckton* (Appleseed, 2004); Dion Fortune, *Glastonbury: Avalon of the Heart* (York Beach, ME: Weiser Books, Inc., 2000).

12   William Kenawell, *The Quest at Glastonbury: a biographical study of Frederick Bligh Bond* (New York: Helix Press, 1965); Frederick Bligh Bond, *The Glastonbury Scripts* (Glastonbury, 1921), 'The story of King Arthur and how he saw the Sangreal, of his institution of the quest of the Holy Grail, and of the promise of the fulfilment of that quest in the latter days: founded on scripts partly metrical received in 1924'. (Glastonbury: *Central Somerset Gazette* 1925).

13   Wood, *Eternal Chalice*, 38–44; Charles Fielding and T. Carr, *The Story of Dion Fortune* (Thoth Publications, 1998).

14   Wood, *Eternal Chalice*, 46–8; James Ussher, *Britannicarum ecclesiarum antiquitates: quibus inserta est ecclesiam inductae haereseos historia* (Collectore Jacobo Usserio Bibliopolarum, 1639) chap. II, 18.

15   Wood, *Eternal Chalice*, 60–70; Juliette Wood, 'The Holy Grail: From Romance Motif to Modern Genre', *Folklore* 111 (2000), 169–190.

16   NLW ex 720. Douglas Hague, Royal Commission on Ancient Monuments in Wales, "Report on Nanteos Cup 16/3/85" Handlist vol. 3, 60, Ceredigion Country Archives *http://www.ceredigion.gov.uk/index.cfm?articleid=10299*.

17 Juliette Wood, 'Nibbling Pilgrims and the Nanteos Cup: A Cardiganshire legend,' 137-50 in *Nanteos A Welsh House and its families*, ed. Gerald Morgan (Llandysul, Gomer, 2001); Ethelwyn M. Amery, *Sought and Found, A Story of the Holy Grail* (1905) rpr. (Aberystwyth, 1910).

18 Wood, 'The Healing Cup of Nanteos', *www.juliettewood.com*.

19 Marion Bowman, 'The Holy Thorn Ceremony Revival: Rivalry and Civil Religion in Glastonbury', *Folklore* 117 (2006), 123–40.

20 Sebastian Evans, *The High History of the Holy Graal*, Temple Classics (London: J. Dent & Co., 1898).

21 Katharine Maltwood, *A Guide to Glastonbury's Temple of the Stars: their giant effigies described from air views, maps, and from 'The high history of the Holy Grail'* (London: John Clarke, 1964).

22 Wood, *Eternal Chalice*, 167–71.

23 W. J. Keith, *A Glastonbury Romance Readers' Guide* 700 (772) (Powys Society, *www.powys-society.org*); Jeremy Hooker, *John Cowper Powys*, Writers of Wales Series (Cardiff: University of Wales Press, 1973).

24 Keith, *A Glastonbury Romance*, 756–7.

5 SECRET GRAILS AND HIDDEN MESSAGES

1 Wood, *Eternal Chalice*, 112–31.

2 Umberto Eco, *Foucault's Pendulum*, William Weaver (tr.) (New York: Harcourt Brace Jovanovich, 1989); Dan Brown, *The Da Vinci Code* (New York: Bantam, 2003); Michael Baigent, Richard Leigh, Henry Lincoln, *The Holy Blood and the Holy Grail* (London: Jonathan Cape, 1982; reissued Corgi 1996), 277–81.

3 Helen Nicholson, *Love, War and the Grail: Templars, Hospitallers, and Teutonic Knights in Medieval Epic and Romance, 1150–1500* (Leiden: Brill, 2001).

4 Nicholson, *The Knights Templar: A New History* (Stroud: Sutton, 2001), 192–3, 207–18; Peter Partner, *The Knights Templar and Their Myth* (Rochester: Destiny Books, 1990), Part II, chaps. 5–8.

5 Robert L. D. Cooper, *The Rosslyn Hoax? Viewing Rosslyn Chapel from a New Perspective* (Lewis, 2006), 36–40, 108–9.

6 Wood, *Eternal Chalice*, 112–38; Partner, *The Knights Templar and Their Myth*, 108–12, 120–9,137–45.

7 Jonathan Sumption, *The Albigensian Crusade* (London: Faber and Faber, 1999), 48–9, 236–41.

8 Barber, *The Holy Grail*, 203–25.

9 Wood, *Eternal Chalice*, 126–8.

10 Nicholas Goodrick-Clarke, *The Occult Roots of Nazism: Secret Aryan Cults and their Influence on Nazi Ideology* (London: I. B. Tauris, 1992), 217–27.

11 Dennis Wheatley, *They Used Dark Forces* (London: Hutchinson, 1964); Duncan Kyle, *Black Camelot* (London: Collins, 1978).

12 *Indiana Jones and the Last Crusade*, Steven Spielberg (dir.), 1989.

13 Michael Baigent, Richard Leigh, Henry Lincoln, *The Holy Blood and the Holy Grail* (reissued Corgi 1996); Wood, *Eternal Chalice*, 107–59.

14 John Hardyng, see above chap. 4, 54–5.

15 Bill Putnam and John Edwin Wood, *The Treasure of Rennes-le-Château: A Mystery Solved* (Stroud: Sutton, 2003, rev. 2005).

16 *www.priory-of-sion.com* is the most comprehensive site associated with the holy bloodline and is updated regularly.

17 Putnam and Wood, *The Accursed Treasure of Rennes-le-Château* (*Le tresor maudit de Rennes-le-Château*), 37–9 (2001).

18 Putnam and Wood, *The Accursed Treasure*, 9–14, 167–74.

19 Wood, *Eternal Chalice*, 147–9.

20 Margaret Starbird, *The Woman with the Alabaster Jar* (Santa Fe: Bear & Co, 1993).

21 Dan Brown, *The Da Vinci Code* (2003); 'Da Vinci code documentaries', *www.priory-of-sion.com*; Sharon Newman, *The Real History Behind the Da Vinci Code* (New York: Berkley Books, 2005).

22 Wood, *Eternal Chalice*, 159–65; *www.shugborough.org.uk/AcademyHome-156*

23 This explanation was first suggested by the archivist at Shugborough in the 1950s. See *www.shugborough.org.uk/AcademyHome-156*.

6 CHAPELS, MONUMENTS AND RELICS

1 Alan Lupack, *The Oxford Guide to Arthurian Legend and Literature* (Oxford: University Press, 2005).

2 Jessie Weston, *Ritual to Romance*, chap. XIII, 'The Perilous Chapel'.

3 Rosslyn Chapel site, *www.rosslynchapel.org.uk*; Lewis Spence, 'Mystical Roslin', *Scottish Motor Traction Magazine* (1952), 29.

4 Wood, *Eternal Chalice*, 131–8; Cooper, *The Rosslyn Hoax?*, 129–71.

5 Andrew Sinclair, *The Sword and the Grail: The Story of the Grail the Templars and the True Discovery of America* (New York: Crown Publishers, 1992); *The Discovery of the Grail* (Century, 1998); *The Secret Scroll* (London: Christopher Sinclair-Stevenson, 2001); *www.rosslyntemplars.org.uk* (accessed 26 December 2006).

6 Jennifer Westwood and Jacqueline Simpson, *The Lore of the Land: A Guide to England's Legends from Spring-Heeled Jack to the Witches of Warboys* (London, Penguin, 2005), 24, 364–5; 415–16, 503–4, 648, 652.

7   Matt. 26:26–8, Mark 14:22–4, Luke 22:17–201, I Cor. 11:25.

8   Barber, *The Holy Grail*, 135–40.

9   Wood, *Eternal Chalice*, 21.

10   Wood, *Eternal Chalice*, 21–6, 'Obscure objects of Desire: Is this the Real Holy Grail?' *www.juliettewood.com*.

11   Barber, *The Holy Grail*, 167–70; Wood, *Eternal Chalice*, 22–7.

12   Wood, *Eternal Chalice*, 38–48; see above chap. 5, 56–61.

13   'The Great Chalice of Antioch: On a Quest for the Holy Grail from Antioch to America and Back Again', *www.juliettewood.com*; Barber, *The Holy Grail*, 300–1.

14   Thomas Costain, *The Silver Chalice* (New York: Doubleday, 1952); *Monty Python and the Holy Grail* (dir. Terry Gilliam, 1975).

15   Barber, *The Holy Grail*, 171–2, 212–17.

16   Wood, *Eternal Chalice*, 167–80.

17   *Lancelot du Lac*, Robert Bresson (dir.) (1974); *Perceval le Gallois*, Eric Rohmer (dir.) (1978); and *Excalibur*, John Boorman (dir.) (1981).

18   *The Light in the Dark* (1922). A shorter version, *The Light of Faith*, appeared soon afterwards.

19   Mary Butts, *Armed with Madness* (London, 1928); Charles Williams, *War In Heaven* (London, 1930).

20   Susan Cooper, *Over Sea, Under Stone* (New York: Harcourt, 1965), *Greenwitch* (New York: Athenaeum, 1975) from *The Dark is Rising*.

SELECT BIBLIOGRAPHY

PRIMARY TEXTS AND TRANSLATIONS

Bliocadran: a Prologue to the Perceval of Chrétien de Troyes, Lenora Wolfgang (ed.) (Tübingen: Niemeyer, 1976).

Chrétien de Troyes, *Perceval the Story of the Grail*, Nigel Bryant (tr.) (Cambridge and Totowa: Brewer, 1982).

The Continuations of the Old French Perceval of Chrétien de Troyes, William Roach (ed.) (Philadelphia: University of Pennsylvania Press, 1949–83).

The Didot Perceval, William Roach (ed.) (Philadelphia: University of Pennsylvania Press, 1971), tr. D. Skeeles (Seattle: University of Washington Press, 1966).

The Elucidation: a Prologue to the Conte del Graal, Albert Wilder Thompson (ed.) (Genève: Slatkine, 1982).

Fouke le Fitz Waryn, E. J. Hathaway et al. (eds) (Oxford: Blackwell, 1975).

The Golden Legend of Jacobus de Voragine, Granger Ryan and Helmut T. Ripperger (tr.) (New York: Arno Press, 1969).

John of Glastonbury, *The Chronicle of Glastonbury Abbey* (*Cronica sive antiquitates Glastoniensis ecclesie*), James P. Carley (ed.), David Townsend (tr.) (Woodbridge, 1985).

The Grail Quest, P. M. Matarasso (ed. and tr.) (Harmondsworth: Penguin, 1969).

Guest, Charlotte, *The Mabinogion from the Llyfr Coch o Hergest and other Ancient Welsh Mss*, 3 vols (London & Llandovery: Longmans, Rees, 1838–49).

Hardyng, John, *The Chronicle of Iohn Hardyng…*, Henry Ellis (ed.) (London: F. C. and J. Rivington, 1812).

Heinrich von dem Türlin, *The Crown* (*Diu Crône*), J. W. Thomas (tr.) (Lincoln and London: University of Nebraska Press, 1989).

Perlesvaus or *The High Book of the Grail*, Nigel Bryant (tr.) (Cambridge: University Press, 1978).

Lancelot-Grail: The Old French Arthurian Vulgate and Post-Vulgate in Translation, Norris J. Lacy (ed.) (New York and London, 1993–6).

Henry Lovelich, *History of the Holy Grail*, F. J. Furnivall (ed.), Early English Text Society, Extra Series (London, 1874–1905).

The Mabinogion, Sioned Davies (tr.) (Oxford University Press, 2007).

Thomas Malory, *Works*, Eugene Vinaver (ed.), P. J. C. Field (rev.) (Oxford: Oxford University Press, 1990).

Merlin and the Grail: Joseph of Arimathea, Merlin and Perceval: the Trilogy of Prose Romances Attributed to Robert de Boron, Nigel Bryant (tr.) (Cambridge and Rochester, 2001).

The Vulgate Version of the Arthurian Romance, H. O. Sommer et al. (eds), 8 vols (repr. New York: The Carnegie Institution, 1979)

William of Malmesbury's *De antiquitate Glastonie Ecclesie* (*The Early History of Glastonbury*), John Scott (ed.) (Woodbridge: Boydell & Brewer, 1981).

Wolfram von Eschenbach, *Parzival*, Cyril Edwards (tr.) (Oxford: University Press, 2006).

Ystoryaeu seint greal, Thomas Jones, J. E. Caerwyn Williams, Ceridwen Lloyd-Morgan, Daniel Huws (eds) (Cardiff: University of Wales Press, 1992).

RESOURCES FOR MODERN GRAIL STUDIES

Amery, Ethelwyn M., *Sought and Found* (n.p. 1905 repr. 1910).

Baigent, Michael, Leigh, Richard, Lincoln, Henry, *The Holy Blood and the Holy Grail* [American edition *Holy Blood Holy Grail*] (London: Jonathan Cape, 1982; reissued Corgi 1996), new edn (London: Century, 2005)

Baigent, Michael, Leigh, Richard, *The Temple and the Lodge* (*c*.1989 repr. London: Arrow, 1998).

Bligh Bond, Frederick, *The Glastonbury Scripts*: Tales of Glastonbury Abbey purporting to be automatic writings (Glastonbury, 1921).

——, 'The story of King Arthur and how he saw the Sangreal, of his institution of the quest of the Holy Grail, and of the promise of the fulfilment of that quest in the latter days' (Glastonbury: *Central Somerset Gazette*, 1925).

Eisen, Gustavus, *The Great Chalice of Antioch*, 2 vols (New York: Konchakji Frères, 1923).

Evans, Sebastian, *The High History of the Holy Graal* (London: J. M. Dent & Co., 1898).

Fortune, Dion, *Glastonbury: Avalon of the Heart* (York Beach, Me, 2000).

Goodchild, John Arthur, *The Light of the West: An Account of the Dannite Settlement in Ireland* (London, 1898).

Graves, Robert, *The White Goddess: a historical grammar of poetic myth*, 1948 new edition by Grevel Lindop (London: Faber and Faber, 1999).

Lewis, Lionel Smithett, *St Joseph of Arimathea at Glastonbury* (repr. 1964) (London: James Clark, 1955).

MacLeod, Fiona (William Sharp), *The Winged Destiny: the Spiritual History of the Gael* (London, 1904).

Machen, Arthur, *The Secret of the Sangraal: a Collection of Writings* (East Sussex: Tartarus Press, 1994).

——, *Things Near and Far* (London: Richards Press, 1951).

Maltwood, Katharine, *King Arthur's Round Table of the Zodiac* (Victoria, B.C.: 1946).

——, *A guide to Glastonbury's Temple of the Stars* (London: John Clarke, 1964).

Starbird, Margaret, *The Woman with the Alabaster Jar: Mary Magdelene and the Holy Grail* (Santa Fe: Bear and Co., 1993).

Ussher, James, *Britannicarum ecclesiarum antiquitates: quibus inserta est ecclesiam inductae haereseos historia* (Collectore Jacobo Usserio Bibliopolarum, 1639).

——, *Strange and Remarkable Prophecies and Predictions: To which is Prefaced a Short Sketch of his Life* (Dublin, 1840).

Sinclair, Andrew, *The Sword and the Grail: The Story of the Grail the Templars and the True Discovery of America* (New York: Crown Publishers, 1992).

——, *The Discovery of the Grail* (London: Century, 1998).

——, *The Secret Scroll* (London: Christopher Sinclair-Stevenson, 2001).

——, *Rosslyn – the Story of Rosslyn Chapel and the True Story behind the Da Vinci Code* (Edinburgh: Birlinn, 2005).

Spence, Lewis, 'Mystical Roslin', *Scottish Motor Traction Magazine* (1952).

Waite, A. E., *The Holy Grail: Its Legends and Symbolism* (London: Rider, 1933).

——, *The Hidden Church of the Holy Grail* (London: Rider, 1909).

INTERNET SOURCES

www.priory-of-sion.com/

www.shugborough.org.uk/AcademyShepherdsMon-169

www.shugborough.org.uk/AcademyHome-156

www.bbc.co.uk/wales/mid/sites/weird/pages/nanteos.shtml

www.aragonesasi.com/libros/santocaliz.php

www.geocities.com/Athens/Rhodes/3946/santocaliz/

www.arch.den.org/dcr/archive/20020911/20029112n.htm

www.juliettewood.com
www.rosslyntemplars.org.uk
www.lib.rochester.edu/camelot/intrvws/cooper.htm

GRAIL LITERATURE AND GAMES

Attanasio, A. A., *Kingdom of the Grail* (New York: Harper, 1992).

Bradley, Marion Zimmer, *The Mists of Avalon* (New York: Knopf, 1982).

Brown, Dan, *The Da Vinci Code* (New York: Bantam, 2003).

Butts, Mary, *Armed with Madness* (London: Wishart & Co., 1928).

Cooper, Susan, *Over Sea Under Stone* (New York: Harcourt, 1965).

——, *Greenwitch* (New York: Athenaeum, 1975).

Cornwell, Bernard, *The Warlord Chronicles: The Winter King, Enemy of God, Excalibur* (London: Penguin, 1995–8).

——, *The Grail Quest: Harlequin, Vagabond, Heretic* (London: HarperCollins, 2000–3).

Costain, Thomas, *The Silver Chalice* (New York: Doubleday, 1952).

Davies, Edward Tegla, *Y Greal Sanctaidd* (Wrecsam: Hughes, 1922).

Eco, Umberto, *Foucault's Pendulum*, William Weaver (tr.) (New York: Harcourt Brace Jovanovich, 1989).

Eliot, T. S., *Collected Poems 1909–1962* (London: Faber and Faber, 1963).

Jensen, Jane, *Gabriel Knight 3: Blood of the Sacred, Blood of the Damned* (Sierra On-Line Games 1996).

Jones, David, *The Anathemata* (London: Faber, 1952).

——, *In Parenthesis* (London: Faber, 1937).

——, *The Sleeping Lord and other Fragments* (London: Faber, 1974).

Kyle, Duncan, *Black Camelot* (London: Collins, 1978).

Lewis, C. S., *That Hideous Strength: A Modern Fairy Tale for Grown-Ups* (London, 1945).

Lowell, James Russell, *The Vision of Sir Launfal* (8th edn) (Boston: Ticknor and Fields, 1863).

Machen, Arthur, *The Secret Glory* (East Sussex: Tartarus Press, 1998).

——, 'The Great Return' in *Holy Terrors: Collected Short Stories* (London: Penguin, 1946).

Miles, Rosalind, *Guenevere, The Child of the Holy Grail* (New York: Simon & Schuster 2000).

Mitchison, Naomi, *To the Chapel Perilous* (London: Allen, 1955).

Mosse, Kate, *Labyrinth* (London: Orion, 2005).

Owen, John Dyfnallt, *Y Greal a Cherddi Eraill* (Gwasg Aberystwyth, 1946).

Parry, Tom, *Saint Greal: y Chwedl Wedi ei Hailadrodd* (Llandysul: Gwasg Gomer, 1933).

Roberts, Dorothy James, *Kinsmen of the Grail* (Boston, Little, 1963).

Rowland, Marcus L, *Queen Victoria and the Holy Grail* (Games Workshop Ltd., 1985).

Southey, James, *The birth lyf and actes of kyng Arthur* [Morte d'Arthur] (London, 1817).

Tennyson, Alfred, *The Holy Grail and Other Poems* (London: Strahan and Co., 1870).

——, *Idyls of the King* (Boston: Ticknor and Fields, 1859).

Williams, Charles, *War In Heaven* (London: Victor Gollanz, 1930).

Wheatley, Dennis, *They Used Dark Forces* (London: Hutchinson, 1964).

TELEVISION AND FILM

'The Lost Treasure of Jerusalem' (1972); 'The Priest the Painter and the Devil' (1974); 'The Shadow of the Templars' (1979), *Chronicle* (BBC2).

The Search for the Holy Grail (BBC2, 1998).

In Search of the Grail (The Learning Channel/Bluebook Films, 2003).

The Real Da Vinci Code (Channel 4, Wildfire Television, 2006).

The Light in the Dark (*The Light of Faith*), Clarence Brown (dir.) (1922).

Lancelot du Lac, Luc Bresson (dir.) (1974).

Monty Python and the Holy Grail, Terry Gilliam and Terry Jones (dir.) (1975).

Perceval Le Gallois, Eric Rohmer (dir.) (1978).

Excalibur, John Boorman (dir.), script by Rospo Pallenberg and John Boorman (1981).

Indiana Jones and the Last Crusade, Steven Spielberg (dir.), script by Jeffrey Boam (1989).

The Fisher King, Terry Gilliam (dir.), script by Richard LaGravenese (1991).

SECONDARY SOURCES AND COMMENTARY

Barber, Richard, *The Holy Grail: Imagination and Belief* (London: Allen Lane, 2004).

Benham, Patrick, *The Avalonians* (Glastonbury: Gothic Image Press, 1993).

Bromwich, Rachel, Jarman, A. O. H., and Roberts, Brynley F. (eds), *The Arthur of the Welsh: The Arthurian Legend in Medieval Welsh Literature* (Cardiff: University of Wales Press, 1991).

John Carey, *Ireland and the Grail* (Aberystwyth: Celtic Studies Publications, 2007).

Carley, James P. (ed.), *Glastonbury Abbey and Arthurian Tradition* (Cambridge: D. S. Brewer, 2001.

Cooper, Robert L. D., *The Rosslyn Hoax? Viewing Rosslyn Chapel from a New Perspective* (Lewis, 2006).

Cox, C. B. and Hinchliffe, Arnold P. (eds), *T. S. Eliot, the Waste Land: A Casebook* (London: Macmillan, 1968).

Cutting, Tracy, *Beneath the Silent Tor: the Life and Work of Alice Buckton* (Great Britain: Appleseed Press, 2004).

Fielding, Charles, and Carr, T., *The Story of Dion Fortune* (Thoth Publications, 1998).

Gentle-Cackett, S. W., *The Antioch Cup* (London, 1935).

Goetinck, Glenys, *Peredur: a Study of Welsh Tradition in the Grail Legends* (Cardiff: University of Wales Press, 1975).

Goodrick Clarke, Nicholas, *The Occult Roots of Nazism: Secret Aryan Cults and their Influence on Nazi Ideology* (London: I. B. Tauris, 1992).

Haskins, Susan, *Mary Magdelen: Myth and Metaphor* (London: HarperCollins, 1993).

Ivakhiv, Adrian J., *Claiming Sacred Ground: Pilgrims and Politics at Glastonbury and Sedona* (Bloomington & Indianapolis, 2001).

Lupack, Alan, *The Oxford Guide to Arthurian Legend and Literature* (Oxford: University Press, 2005).

Kenawell, William, *The Quest at Glastonbury: A Biographical Study of Frederick Bligh Bond* (New York: Helix Press, 1965).

Lacey, Norris J., *The New Arthurian Encyclopaedia* (Chicago and London 1991).

Loomis, R. S., *Celtic Myth and Arthurian Romance* (New York: Columbia Press, 1927, rev. 1935).

——, *Arthurian Tradition and Chrétien de Troyes* (New York: Columbia University Press, 1949).

——, *Wales and the Arthurian Legend* (Cardiff: University of Wales Press, 1956).

——, *The Grail: From Celtic Myth to Christian Symbol* (Cardiff: University of Wales Press, 1963).

Mahony, Dhira B, *The Grail: A Casebook* (New York: Garland, 2000).

Marino, John B., *The Grail Legend in Modern Literature*, Arthurian Studies LIX (Cambridge: Boydell & Brewer, 2004).

Newman, Sharan, *The Real History Behind the Da Vinci Code* (New York: Berkley Books, 2005).

Nicholson, Helen, *Love, War and the Grail: Templars, Hospitallers, and Teutonic Knights in Medieval Epic and Romance, 1150–1500* (Leiden: Brill, 2001).

——, *The Knights Templar: A New History* (Stroud: Sutton, 2001).

Nutt, Alfred, *Studies in the Legend of the Holy Grail: with especial reference to the hypothesis of its Celtic origin* (London: David Nutt, 1888).

——, *Legends of the Holy Grail* (London: David Nutt, 1902).

Putnam, Bill and John Edwin Wood, *The Treasure of Rennes-le-Château: A Mystery Solved* (Stroud: Sutton, 2003, rev. 2005).

Robinson, J. Armitage, *Two Glastonbury Legends: King Arthur and St Joseph of Arimathea* (Cambridge, 1926).

Lawrence Schick, *Heroic Worlds: A History and Guide to Role-playing Games* (New York: Prometheus Press, 1991).

Sumption, Jonathan, *The Albigensian Crusade* (London: Faber and Faber, 1999).

Treharne, R. F., *The Glastonbury Legends: Joseph of Arimathea, the Holy Grail and King Arthur* (London, 1967).

Weston, Jessie Laidley, 'The Grail and the Rites of Adonis', *Folklore* 18 (1907), 283–305.

——, *From Ritual to Romance*, 1925 repr. (Princeton: Princeton University Press, 1993).

Westwood, Jennifer and Simpson, Jacqueline, *The Lore of the Land: A Guide to England's Legends* (London, Penguin, 2005).

Wood, Juliette, 'The Creation of the Celtic Tarot', *Folklore* 109 (1998), 15–24.

——, *Eternal Chalice: the enduring legend of the Holy Grail* (London: I. B. Tauris, 2008).

——, 'Folklore Studies at the Celtic Dawn: Alfred Nutt: Publisher and Folklorist', *Folklore* 110 (1999), 3–12.

——, 'Nibbling Pilgrims and the Nanteos Cup: A Cardiganshire Legend', 137–150 in *Nanteos: A Welsh House and its Families*, Gerald Morgan (ed.) (Llandysul: Gomer, 2001).

——, 'The Holy Grail: From Romance Motif to Modern Genre', *Folklore* 111 (2000), 169–190.

——, 'A Welsh Triad: Charlotte Guest, Marie Trevelyan, Mary Williams', 259–76 in *Women & Tradition: A Neglected Group of Folklorists*, Carmen Blacker & Hilda Davidson (eds) (Durham, North Carolina: Carolina Academic Press, 2000).

INDEX